P9-DIZ-518

A Field Guide to the Birds
was first published on April 27, 1934.
This reprint of that edition commemorates
the life and work of
ROGER TORY PETERSON
(August 28, 1908–July 28, 1996).

A FIELD GUIDE TO THE BIRDS

GIVING FIELD MARKS OF ALL SPECIES
FOUND IN EASTERN NORTH AMERICA

TEXT AND ILLUSTRATIONS
IN COLOR AND IN BLACK AND WHITE

BY
ROGER TORY PETERSON

BOSTON AND NEW YORK
HOUGHTON MIFFLIN COMPANY
The Riverside Press Cambridge
1934

COPYRIGHT, 1934, BY ROGER T. PETERSON
COPYRIGHT © 1961 BY ROGER TORY PETERSON

ALL RIGHTS RESERVED INCLUDING THE RIGHT TO REPRODUCE
THIS BOOK OR PARTS THEREOF IN ANY FORM

CIP DATA IS AVAILABLE.

The Riverside Press
CAMBRIDGE · MASSACHUSETTS
PRINTED IN THE U.S.A.

TO

CLARENCE E. ALLEN

AND

WILLIAM VOGT

PREFACE

THOSE of us who have read Ernest Thompson Seton's 'Two Little Savages' remember, perhaps as well as anything contained within the two covers of that informative volume, the trip made by Yan to the hotel at Downey's Dump and the pattern charts he made of the mounted ducks he found there.

This lad had a book that showed him how to tell ducks when they were *in the hand*, but since he only saw the live birds at a distance, he was frequently at a loss for their names. He noticed, however, that all ducks were different — all had little blotches or streaks that were their labels or indentification tags. He deduced then, that if he could put their labels or "uniforms" down on paper, he would know the ducks as soon as he saw them on the water.

Many of us, later on, when the sport of bird-study first revealed its pleasurable possibilities, tried to locate a book — a guide — that would treat *all* birds in the manner that Yan and the ducks had suggested. We found many volumes covering the whole field of ornithology. But although descriptions were complete and illustrations authoritative, the one thing we wished for — a 'boiling-down,' or simplification, of things so that any bird could be readily and surely told *from all the others* at a glance or at a distance — that, except fragmentarily, we were unable to find.

We would study a colored plate of Warblers, thorough in its treatment of dull-colored juveniles and autumn plumages, but confusing in the similarity of them all. We would select some point on each bird as being perhaps the diagnostic feature, though we could not be certain. Fancied differences were noted, while the really distinctive characteristics were overlooked. This shadow of uncertainty that darkened many of our earlier finds of 'rare' birds marred our enjoyment of the study.

Hence this handbook — designed to complement the standard ornithological works, a guide to the field-marks of Eastern birds, wherein live birds may be run down by impressions, patterns, and distinctive marks, rather than by the anatomical differences and measurements that the collector would find useful.

Those who have been fortunate enough to go on trips with Mr. Charles A. Urner, of Elizabeth, New Jersey, will agree that he is truly phenomenal in his ability afield. I wish to express my gratitude to him for a criticism of a large part of the text and illustrations, especially those sections dealing with the water-birds.

Dr. John B. May, of Cohasset, Massachusetts, has examined the manuscript and has helped with a number of suggestions, especially concerning the Hawks and Owls — the two groups in which lie his especial interest.

Mr. Francis H. Allen, of Boston, who for many years has been one of the most active and observant of field enthusiasts in New England, has contributed a number of valuable notes and is responsible for a complete perusal and polishing-off of the text.

As it is quite generally and rightfully agreed that Mr. Ludlow Griscom, of Cambridge, is a court of last resort in matters of field identification, I have turned to him for a final criticism of the text and illustrations, which he has graciously given. The responsibility for any errors of omission or commission is, however, the author's.

To the following I am also indebted, for notes, suggestions, and other aid: — Miss Phyllis M. Bergen, T. Donald Carter, S. Gilbert Emilio, William G. Fargo, John F. Kuerzi, Joseph Hickey, Francis Lee Jaques, John T. Nichols, Mark C. Rich, Charles H. Rogers, and Alexander Sprunt, Jr.

Mr. James L. Peters has been of kind assistance in guiding me about the splendid skin-collections of the Museum of Comparative Zoölogy at Cambridge, Massachusetts. Mr. John D. Smith, of the Museum of the Boston Society of Natural History, has given access to the interesting material over which he presides. For the use of their collections I am also indebted to the American Museum of Natural History in New York City and the Natural History Museum of Buffalo, New York.

References were made to the following works: Chapman's *Handbook of Birds of Eastern North America*, Alexander's

Birds of the Ocean, Bent's *Life Histories of North American Birds,* Phillips's *Natural History of the Ducks,* Coward's *Birds of the British Isles and Their Eggs,* Taverner's *Birds of Western Canada,* Dawson's *Birds of California,* Roberts's *Birds of Minnesota,* Hoffmann's *Guide to the Birds,* Forbush's *Birds of Massachusetts and other New England States,* Eaton's *Birds of New York,* Griscom's *Birds of the New York City Region,* Wayne's *Birds of South Carolina,* and Howell's *Florida Bird Life.*

Without the highly appreciated prompting or the constant criticism and help of William Vogt, of the Jones Beach State Bird Sanctuary, Long Island, this guide would probably never have been undertaken nor completed.

CONTENTS

ILLUSTRATIONS

HOW TO USE THIS BOOK

VETERANS in the field study of birds will need no suggestions as to ways of using this book. Beginners, however, will do well to bear in mind a few comments that will point to short cuts. A few moments should be spent in familiarizing one's self, in a general way, with the illustrations; the briefest examination of the plates will be sufficient to give the beginner an idea of the shapes of our birds and the groups to which they belong. Ducks, it will be seen, do not resemble Loons; and the Gulls will be readily separable from the Terns. The needle-like bills of the Warblers will immediately distinguish them from the seed-cracking bills of the Sparrows. Birds of a kind — that is, birds that could be confused — are grouped together where easy comparison is possible. Thus, when a bird has been seen in the field, the observer can immediately turn to the picture most resembling it and feel confident that he has reduced the possibilities to the few species in its own group.

In many instances the pictures tell the story without help from the letterpress. This is true of such plates as those illustrating the Swallows, the Vireos, the Thrushes, the diving birds, etc. In every case, however, it is well to check identifications from the drawings by referring to the text. The plates give visual field-marks that may be used in comparing and sorting out species seen in life. The text gives field-marks, such as range, habits, manner of flight, etc., that could not be pictured, and, in addition, mentions the birds that might, in any instance, be confused with a given species.

In cases where the plates, without the text, do not give definitive identifications, the observer should select the picture that most resembles the bird he saw, and then consult the text. We may, for example, be puzzled by a bird that is certainly a female Merganser. A consultation of the brief descriptions of those birds eliminates the Hooded Merganser because the bird sought had a reddish head — not a dark one. It was seen on the coast which, so the text tells us, increases the *probability* it was a Red-breast. And finally, we learn that in the Red-breasted Merganser 'the rufous of the head *blends* into the white of the throat and neck instead of being sharply defined' as in the American Merganser. This characteristic, which accurately describes the bird we have seen, makes the identification certain. This soft merging of color is clearly shown in the plate but because we had not known what to look for, we failed to notice it.

Far from helping only the beginner who can scarcely tell a Gull from a Duck, it is hoped that the advanced student will find this guide comprehensive enough to be of service in recognizing those accidentals or rarities that sometimes appear in the territory he knows so thoroughly.

Some of the assertions herein contained, of the ease with which certain birds may be distinguished, will possibly be questioned on the ground that older works have stated that they are 'very difficult' or 'impossible' to identify except in the hand.

Doubting Thomases need but take a few trips afield with some of our present-day experts in field identifications — of whom Ludlow Griscom is one of the most outstanding examples — to realize the possibility of quickly identifying almost any bird, with amazing certainty, at the snap of a finger. It is but a matter of seeing a bird often enough and knowing exactly what to look for, to be able to distinguish, with a very few exceptions, even the most confusing forms.

Most of the 'rare finds' are made by people who are alive to the possibilities and know what to look for should they detect anything unusual. It is the discovery of rarities that puts real zest into the sport of birding, a zest that many of us would like to interpret as 'scientific zeal' rather than the quickening of our sporting blood.

Field birding as most of us engage in it is a game — a most absorbing game. As we become more proficient, we attempt to list as many birds as we can in a day. The May 'big day' or ' century run,' where the day's goal is a hundred species or more, is the apogee of this sort of thing.

Old-timers minimize the scientific value of this type of bird work. Truly, it has but little. Recognition is not the end and aim of ornithology, but is certainly a most fascinating diversion — and a stage through which the person who desires to contribute to our knowledge of ornithology might profitably pass.

The Illustrations. The plates and cuts scattered throughout the text are intended as diagrams, arranged so that quick, easy comparison can be made of the species that most resemble one another. As they are not intended to be pictures or portraits, all modelling of form and feathering is eliminated where it can be managed, so that simple contour and pattern remain. Even color is often an unnecessary, if not, indeed, a confusing, factor. In many of the waterfowl, which we seldom see at close range, this is especially true; so most of the diagrams are carried out in black and white. With many of the small birds, however, since color is quite essential to identification, a departure from the monochrome in the illustrations is necessarily made.

Although the overhead flight patterns of hawks had been worked out years ago, notably by Ernest Thompson Seton, Dr. John B. May, in Forbush's *Birds of Massachusetts*, was the first to revive and popularize the idea. There could hardly be a superior manner of presenting them for study.

Area. The area covered by this book is, as in Dr. Chapman's classic *Handbook*, North America east of the ninetieth meridian. Those few European forms which occur in Greenland but never on the American continent proper are excluded, as are a few of the accidentals that have occurred but once or so and might never be recorded again. Others that have been recorded only two or three times, but might reasonably be expected to be found again in the future, especially the well-marked, recognizable forms, are included.

Song. Song description, except where it may be of distinct service in the initial identification of a bird, is dispensed with. We make our first identification of a species, as a rule, by sight; then we become familiar with its song.

A 'sizzling trill' or a 'bubbling warble' conveys but a wretched idea of the real effect produced by the voice of any particular bird. They are descriptions, but are of little help — except in remembering a note we have already identified. Word syllabifications are even worse. Imagine fitting the Song Sparrow's tune to words as some ornithological writers have attempted to do! However, there are a few species with interpretable songs that we seldom see before we know them quite well by sound. Who has known the Whip-poor-will before hearing its cry at night, or the Oven-bird before its *teacher-teacher-teacher* was familiar?

Then there are those few, such as the small Flycatchers, that are far more easily recognized by voice than by appearance. These pages, then, will treat the songs and notes only when it seems definitely helpful.

Identification by Elimination. Identification by elimination plays an important part in field work. For example, three very similar birds — the Acadian, the Nelson's, and the common Sharp-tailed Sparrows — are found in the Eastern United States. On Lake Erie only one of them occurs — the Nelson's. The student in that region, knowing this, ceases to bother about the other two, once having ascertained the bird in question to be a Sharp-tail.

A thorough acquaintance with any existing State or local lists should properly be made by the beginner. The importance of these lists can hardly be stressed too much. This handbook does not attempt to give a detailed account of the range of each species.

Identification by elimination has many other phases. A Sharp-tailed Sparrow is in the field of our glass with its back turned. The back is contrastingly striped with brown and white; that eliminates the pale-backed Acadian subspecies. The bird faces about; a buffy breast almost devoid of obvious streaks presents itself. By experience — or consultation of the plates — we know that the common Sharp-tail always shows conspicuous sharp breast markings. Hence, our bird must be the Nelson's Sparrow. It is often quite as helpful to know what a bird could not be as what it might be.

In like manner there might be elimination by season. On Long Island all the Sharp-tails might occur in migration, but in midsummer any Sharp-tail seen could be called, with an extremely high degree of probability, the common variety. Here again, the value of a local list is evident.

Caution in Sight Records. It need hardly be pointed out that identification by elimination might have its dangers. One should always use a certain amount of caution in making sight identifications, especially where rarities are concerned.

The ornithologist of the old school seldom accepted a sight record unless it was made along the barrel of a shotgun. Today it is difficult for the average person to secure collecting privileges; moreover, a large proportion of the real rarities show up in parks, preserves, sanctuaries, or on municipal property where collecting is out of the question. There is no reason why we should not trust our eyes — at least after we have acquired a good basic knowledge of the commoner species. Caution should be the keynote. A quick field observer who does not temper his snap judgment with a bit of caution is like a fast car without brakes.

A FIELD GUIDE TO
THE BIRDS

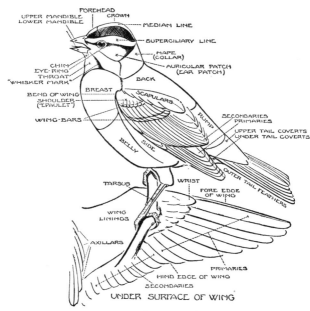

TOPOGRAPHY OF A BIRD

Showing the terms used in this volume

A FIELD GUIDE TO
THE BIRDS

LOONS: GAVIIDÆ

LARGE swimming birds, much larger than Ducks and with shorter necks than Geese. The sharp-pointed bill is a diagnostic feature. Like the Grebes, they are expert divers.

COMMON LOON. *Gavia immer.*
Size of a small Goose.
Breeding plumage: — Head and neck glossy black; back checkered with black and white; under parts white. The adult in the black and white plumage is unmistakable.
Winter plumage: — Mostly grayish; top of head, back of neck, and back dark gray; cheek, throat, and under parts white.
In flight the Loons appear like big Mergansers with legs trailing out behind, but with much slower wing-beats than any Duck. On the water, they appear to be long-bodied, low-lying birds. Sometimes they swim with only the head and neck above water. They somewhat resemble the Cormorants at a distance. A Cormorant would be much blacker than a Loon, especially in winter, and in flight its longer neck and tail and faster wing-beats would be quite evident. On the water the Cormorant swims with its bill pointed slightly upward at an angle.

PACIFIC LOON. *Gavia arctica pacifica.*
Quite accidental in the Eastern States. Similar in size to the Red-throated Loon.
Breeding plumage: — The *gray* hind-neck and black throat make good field marks.
Winter plumage: — As it is so similar to the other Loons at

this season, it should be recorded only if collected. This bird will appear about the size of the Red-throated Loon, but will lack the *speckled* back of the latter species. Instead, the markings of the back have a scaly effect. The bill is quite as slender as that of the Red-throat, *but not upturned.*

RED-THROATED LOON. *Gavia stellata.*
Smaller than the Common Loon; nearer the size of a Merganser.
Breeding plumage: — In summer plumage this species, with its gray head and *rufous-red* throat-patch, is unmistakable, but it is seldom seen in this plumage in our waters.
Winter plumage: — This is the plumage in which we most often see this bird. Mainly *grayish* and white in color, like the Common Loon, but the back is *spotted* with white, giving the bird a paler appearance at long range. The gray on the head and hind-neck of this species is pale, merging into the white and offering none of the black and white contrast of the Common Loon.
The appearance of the bills of the two birds is the *best* index to their identity. The bill of the Red-throat is more slender and seems to be slightly *upturned*, a character that is apparent at a considerable distance. The bill of the Common Loon is stouter and straighter.
Another good point is the snaky profile of the present species.

GREBES: COLYMBIDÆ

The Grebes are Ducklike swimming water-birds; poor fliers but expert divers. They may be distinguished from the Ducks by the pointed bill, narrow head and neck, and tailless appearance. The Grebes normally hold their necks quite erect; Loons and Ducks do so only when alarmed.

HOLBOELL'S GREBE. *Colymbus griseigena holboelli.*
This species is much larger than our other Eastern Grebes, being as large as a fair-sized Duck.
Breeding plumage: — Body of bird gray, shading to white below; neck rufous-red; cheeks white; crown black; bill yellow.

HORNED GREBE

SUMMER   WINTER

PIED BILLED GREBE

SUMMER

HOLBOELL'S GREBE

SUMMER   WINTER

WESTERN GREBE

RED THROATED LOON

SUMMER   WINTER

COMMON LOON

SUMMER   WINTER

Winter plumage: — This is the plumage in which the bird is best known to most people in the United States. Generally grayish in color; top of head darker; *conspicuous white crescent-shaped mark* on the side of the head. In flight the bird shows two white patches on each wing. There are three species of birds found in the same waters as this species during the colder months with which it is often confused.

The Holboell's Grebe may be separated from the Horned Grebe by its larger size, much heavier head, neck, and bill, and more uniform gray coloration. (The Horned Grebe has contrasting white cheeks and a white neck.) It can be distinguished from the Red-throated Loon at long range by its grayer face and neck. The Loon, on the water, at a distance, appears as a long-bodied bird with a proportionately shorter neck, whereas the Grebe is a shorter-bodied bird that seems to be all head and neck. In flight, at a distance, this Grebe resembles the female Red-breasted Merganser, but it beats its wings more slowly, has two white patches on each wing instead of one, and holds its neck bent slightly downward — this last a very good field character. The Merganser flies with its neck and body held perfectly horizontal.

HORNED GREBE. *Colymbus auritus.*
A small Grebe, most typical of the lakes, bays, and open bodies of water.
Breeding plumage: — Head black, with conspicuous buff-colored ear-tufts; neck and flanks rufous-red; back gray; under parts white.
Winter plumage: — Contrastingly patterned with dark gray and white. Top of head, line down back of neck, and back dark gray; under parts, neck, and cheeks clear white and sharply defined.

WESTERN GREBE. *Æchmophorus occidentalis.*
This bird is purely accidental in the eastern United States and should be identified with extreme care.
Larger than the Holboell's Grebe, with an extremely long slender neck. In any plumage it is an all *black and white* bird. Top of head, line on back of neck, and back, black; cheeks, neck, and under parts, white. The presence of only one white

wing-patch will positively separate it from the Holboell's Grebe, which has two white patches on each wing.

Pied-Billed Grebe. *Podilymbus podiceps podiceps.*
The common Grebe of the ponds, creeks, and marshes; the breeding Grebe of the eastern United States.
Breeding plumage: — Gray-brown, darkest on top of the head and the back; throat-patch and spot across bill black.
Winter plumage: — Browner, without the black throat-patch and bill-mark.
The thick, *rounded* bill of the Pied-bill will distinguish it in profile at a distance, in any plumage, from the Horned Grebe with its slender, pointed bill. The Pied-bill has *no white* in the wing as have the others of the group.

SHEARWATERS: PUFFININÆ

Gull-like sea-birds; uniform sooty brown, or two-toned — brown above and white below. The flight of the Shearwaters, several flaps and a sail, is quite distinctive. By comparison with a Gull, a Shearwater's wings are narrow proportionately and the tail is not so fanlike.

Sooty Shearwater. *Puffinus griseus.*
Uniform dark dusky brown; under surface of wings paler.
Since at a distance the Sooty Shearwater looks all black, it can hardly be confused with any other Gull-like sea-bird. Dark Jaegers always show white at the base of the primaries.

Audubon's Shearwater. *Puffinus lherminieri.*
A very small Shearwater, not much more than half the size of the Greater Shearwater, or about twelve inches; found off the Atlantic coast of the Southern States. It resembles the Greater Shearwater in pattern, black above and white below, the black of the top of the head contrasting strikingly with the white of the throat, as in that species, but it does not show any white ring at the base of the tail.

Greater Shearwater. *Puffinus gravis.*
The commonest species of the group. Slightly smaller than the Herring Gull.

Dusky brown above, white below; top of head blackish, sharply defined against the white of the throat; white ring at base of tail; bill black.

Large Gull-like birds, dark above and white below, flapping and sailing over the surface of the water, are very likely to be this species. The *sharply separated* black and white coloration of the head distinguishes it at once from the paler Cory's Shearwater.

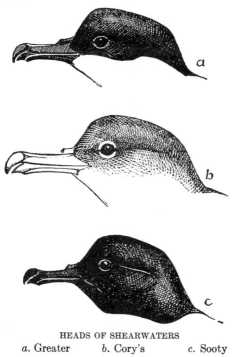

HEADS OF SHEARWATERS

a. Greater   *b.* Cory's   *c.* Sooty

CORY'S SHEARWATER. *Puffinus diomedea borealis.*

Similar to the Greater Shearwater, but larger and **paler.** The *gray* color of the top of the head *blends* into the white of the throat, whereas in the Greater Shearwater the black cap and the white are sharply defined. The bill of the Cory's Shearwater is yellow, whereas the Greater Shearwater's bill is black.

MEDITERRANEAN SHEARWATER. *Puffinus diomedea diomedea.*

A smaller form of the Cory's Shearwater occasionally found on this side of the Atlantic. Characterized by white on the inner webs of the outer primaries. (Do not confuse with Jaegers.)

FULMARS: FULMARINÆ

Gull-like birds, similar to, but more robust than, Shearwaters.

FULMAR. *Fulmarus glacialis glacialis.*

The Fulmar is a bird of the colder parts of the North Atlantic, occurring off the United States only on the fishing-banks off the New England coast during the colder months.

Slightly smaller than the Herring Gull.

Light phase: — Head and under parts white; back and wings gray; wings darker towards the tips; bill yellow. The Fulmar resembles the Herring Gull in this phase, but its manner of flight is different. The wings are held quite straight, and the bird sails over the water more in the manner of a Shearwater. The Fulmar lacks the sharply defined black wing-tips of the Gull.

Dark phase: — Uniform smoky gray; wing-tips darker; bill yellow. In this plumage the bird resembles the Sooty Shearwater but is much paler in color.

The Fulmar's bill is shorter than the Shearwater's, giving a Dovelike appearance to the head.

STORM PETRELS: HYDROBATIDÆ

These Petrels are the little black birds with white rump-patches that flit over the surface of the water in the wake of ocean-going vessels. A number of species have been recorded in eastern North America, but most of them have appeared accidentally, on but one or more occasions, and would be very

BROWN PELICAN

MAN·O'·WAR· BIRD

MALE

IMMATURE

ADULT GANNET

WHITE· BELLIED BOOBY

YELLOW·BILLED TROPIC·BIRD

IMMATURE EUROPEAN CORMORANT

SKUA

DOUBLE·CRESTED CORMORANT

ADULT

LIGHT

DARK

FULMAR

unlikely to fall under ordinary field observation. Thus only our two common kinds will be considered.

LEACH'S PETREL. *Oceanodroma leucorhoa leucorhoa.*
The breeding Petrel of the North Atlantic. About the size of a Purple Martin.

Dark dusky brown; wing-coverts light brown; rump-patch white; feet black; *tail forked.*

The Leach's Petrel is decidedly browner than the more abundant Wilson's Petrel, has a forked tail, and much shorter legs. It has a more *bounding, butterfly-like* flight that will mark it at a long distance — its best field character.

PETRELS
a. Wilson's   *b.* Leach's

WILSON'S PETREL. *Oceanites oceanicus.*
Slightly smaller than the Purple Martin.

Black, with a conspicuous white rump-patch; tail even at end. The yellow-webbed feet extend beyond the tail's tip.

As the Wilson's Petrel is far commoner off our shores than the Leach's, except in Maine and farther north, most sight records of Petrels are automatically referred to this species.

TROPIC-BIRDS: PHAËTHONTIDÆ

YELLOW-BILLED TROPIC-BIRD. *Phaëthon lepturus catesbyi.*
Like the Petrels, Tropic-birds spend most of their life far out at sea, beating on strong, quick wings over the trackless water. They are somewhat smaller than the Herring Gull,

largely white, with two extremely long *central tail-feathers* — so long and streaming that they distinguish *Phaëthon* from all other sea-birds. The tails could be more easily compared (in length) to those of the Scissor-tailed Flycatcher than to the needle-pointed feathers of the Terns. The present species, the 'Long-tail,' which breeds in Bermuda, is the only one that would (on rare occasions) be likely to be observed off our Atlantic Coast. The rapid pigeon-like flight and the long tails are distinctive. Sometimes they sit on the water, riding high with the tails held well clear.

PELICANS: PELECANIDÆ

Extremely large water-birds with long flat bills and tremendous throat-pouches. Pelicans fly low in orderly lines, alternating several flaps with a short sail, each bird in the flock playing follow-my-leader, flapping and sailing in rhythm, apparently taking the cue from the bird in front. They do not fly with necks outstretched as do most large water-birds, but draw their heads back on their shoulders.

WHITE PELICAN. *Pelecanus erythrorhynchos.*
A huge white bird with black primaries and a great yellow throat-patch.
No other large white bird is at all like it; Swans have no black wing-tips; the Wood Ibis has black primaries, but flies with neck extended and long legs trailing.

BROWN PELICAN. *Pelecanus occidentalis occidentalis.*
A ponderous dark water-bird with more or less white about the head and neck (in adults). Flies with its head hunched back on its shoulders and its long flat bill resting comfortably on its curved neck.
Its size and flight, a few flaps and a sail, proclaim it a pelican; its dusky color at once eliminates its white relative.

GANNETS AND BOOBIES: SULIDÆ

Very large Gull-like sea-birds with much longer necks and larger bills than Gulls. As the Gannet is the only one of the group normally found on the Atlantic Coast of the United

States, it is proper that it be the basis of comparison for the more or less accidental members of the family.

GANNET. *Moris bassana.*

Great white birds with broad blackish wing-tips wheeling in wide circles over the waves are quite certainly Gannets. They are twice the size of Herring Gulls, with much longer necks and larger bills, which are carried pointed toward the water, and pointed, not fan-shaped, tails. One seldom sees them close enough to observe these details. When fishing over the sea, they drop Kingfisher-like into the waves, sending a spout of sudsy foam high in the air. Gulls sometimes plunge from the air into the water, either in play or for food, but the plunge is by no means spectacular.

Young birds are dusky all over, but shape and actions will identify them. Sometimes young spring birds are mottled, with dark heads.

ATLANTIC BLUE-FACED BOOBY. *Sula dactylatra dactylatra.*
A white Booby, or Gannet-like bird, with a *black tail.*

WHITE-BELLIED BOOBY. *Sula leucogaster.*
A *blackish* Booby with a *clear white belly,* in clean-cut contrast to a dark breast.

A young Gannet would not show the well-defined contrast of white belly and dark breast. Immature birds would resemble young Gannets more closely, but would be much blacker, with yellow feet.

RED-FOOTED BOOBY. *Sula piscator.*
A small white Booby with *entirely black wings.*

Young birds are brown, but in any stage of plumage would show silvery wing quills.

CORMORANTS: PHALACROCORACIDÆ

Large, dark water-birds, much larger than any of the Ducks. To be confused only with the Loons, or possibly young Gannets, but for the longer neck, long tail, and fast-beating wings. In flight, the neck is held slightly above the horizontal.

Loons have a much slower wing-beat. Of course, in winter, when Loons are paler, Cormorants can be told by their very blackness, especially the adults, which are black beneath as well as above. Loons are always clear white below. Flocks usually fly in line or wedge formation very much like Geese. Cormorants are sometimes called 'Nigger Geese.' A large dark bird perched in an *upright position* on some rock or buoy over the water can hardly be anything else. On the water they lie low like Loons, but their necks appear more erect and snakelike, and their bills point upwards *at an angle*.

EUROPEAN CORMORANT. *Phalacrocorax carbo carbo.*

Most of the Cormorants seen in midwinter on New England shores can be automatically assigned to this species. It is a much larger bird than the commoner Double-crest, but unless comparison is available, size cannot be relied upon.

The adult at close range shows a *white throat-patch* bordering the yellow chin-pouch, and in spring has a small white patch on the flanks. The chin-pouch of the Double-crest is more orange.

Immature birds are whiter below than the Double-crest, the white extending clear to the under tail-coverts. The dingier white of the other bird blends into black on the lower belly.

DOUBLE-CRESTED CORMORANT. *Phalacrocorax auritus auritus.*

The common Cormorant of the North Atlantic Coast, and the only one of the family likely to be found in the interior. (See remarks under Cormorants and European Cormorant, above.)

FLORIDA CORMORANT. *Phalacrocorax auritus floridanus.*

A slightly smaller form of the Double-crest; the breeding Cormorant of the South Atlantic Coast from North Carolina southward, and westward along the Gulf.

MEXICAN CORMORANT. *Phalacrocorax olivaceus mexicanus.*

A Gulf Coast species, similar to the Florida Double-crest, but considerably smaller; face and pouch bordered by white in the breeding-season.

DARTERS: ANHINGIDÆ

WATER-TURKEY. *Anhinga anhinga.*

Timbered swamps and forest-rimmed pools in the South are the home of the Water-Turkey, or, as it is variously called, Snake-bird or Anhinga.

It is mainly blackish with large silvery patches on the fore part of the wings, and with a long tail and a long, serpentine neck; it perches similarly to a Cormorant, in upright posture, on some dead tree or snag, but the neck is so much snakier than that bird that they should not be confused. In flight it progresses with alternate flapping and sailing, the slender neck extended in front, the long tail spread fanwise. The Anhinga spends much of the day soaring about high over its home swamps.

MAN–O'–WAR BIRDS: FREGATIDÆ.

MAN-O'-WAR BIRD. *Fregata magnificens.*

Voyagers in warmer seas may often see great long-winged black birds, with forked Barn-Swallow-like tails, soaring with the greatest ease in the face of the wind. These are the Man-o'-Wars, or Frigate-Birds. Their wings are longer in proportion to the body-bulk than those of any other sea-bird.

The male is entirely black, with an orange throat-patch; the female has a white breast; and the immature has the whole head and under parts white.

HERONS AND BITTERNS: ARDEIDÆ

Long-legged, long-necked wading birds with long sharp-pointed bills. In sustained flight their heads are drawn back to their shoulders. Cranes and Ibises, which are otherwise quite Heron-like, fly with necks outstretched.

GREAT WHITE HERON. *Ardea occidentalis.*

A large white Heron, larger than an Egret, or about the size of a Great Blue. The bill is yellow, like that of the American Egret, but instead of dark, blackish legs, the legs are *yellowish.*

WÜRDEMANN'S HERON.

A hybrid between the Ward's Great Blue Heron, and the

Great White Heron; like a **Ward's** Heron with a pure white head, lacking the black plume.

CRANES AND IBISES FLY WITH NECKS EXTENDED; HERONS, WITH NECKS PULLED IN

a. Sandhill Crane   *b.* Wood Ibis   *c.* Great Blue Heron

GREAT BLUE HERON. *Ardea herodias herodias.*

This great bird, the 'crane' of the country boy, stands about four feet tall, and is, next to the Sandhill Crane, the largest

BLACK-CROWNED
NIGHT HERON

ADULT

IMMATURE

AMERICAN
BITTERN

LEAST BITTERN

YELLOW-CROWNED
NIGHT HERON
ADULT

GREEN HERON
ADULT

GREAT BLUE HERON

LITTLE BLUE HERON
ADULT

LITTLE BLUE HERON
IMMATURE

AMERICAN EGRET

SNOWY EGRET

LOUISIANA
HERON

HERONS
AND
BITTERNS

wading bird found in the Northern States. Its long legs, long neck, and sharp-pointed bill, and, in flight, its drawn-in neck, will mark the bird as a Heron. The great size and the blue-gray coloration, whiter about the head and neck, will identify it as this species.

WARD'S HERON. *Ardea herodias wardi.*

The breeding Great Blue Heron of the South, from southeast South Carolina, southern Alabama, and southeast Illinois to the Gulf and the Florida Keys. Larger and paler than the Great Blue Heron, with *greenish* instead of black legs and a much whiter head.

AMERICAN EGRET. *Casmerodius albus egretta.*

A large Heron of snowy-white plumage, with black legs and feet and a *yellow bill.*

The Snowy Egret and the immature Little Blue Heron are also white, but are much smaller and have black or blackish bills instead of yellow.

SNOWY EGRET. *Egretta thula thula.*

A medium-sized white Heron with a black bill, black legs, and *yellow feet.* The American Egret is much larger and has a yellow bill and black feet, almost the reverse in color of those parts in the Snowy. The Little Blue Heron in the white plumage is about the same size as the Snowy, but has a touch of blue in the primaries and does not have yellow feet. A young Snowy, before its feet have become yellow, could be identified only at close range, when the lack of bluish in the primaries could be noted. It will be observed that when feeding this species shuffles about with its feet so as to stir up the food, a habit not noticeable in the other white Herons.

REDDISH EGRET. *Dichromanassa rufescens rufescens.*

A medium-sized Heron, larger than a Little Blue Heron, with a heavier bill.

The normal phase is neutral gray, with a buffy-brown head and neck, and a *flesh-colored, black-tipped bill.*

In the scarcer white phase it appears like an American Egret, but it is shorter and stouter, the legs are *blue,* and in flight the wing-strokes are not so deep and slow. The only *necessary* recognition mark to be remembered for either plumage is the flesh-colored, black-tipped bill.

LOUISIANA HERON. *Hydranassa tricolor ruficollis.*

A slender medium-sized Heron, dark in color, with a clear white belly. The contrasting white belly is the key-mark in any plumage.

LITTLE BLUE HERON. *Florida cærulea cærulea.*

A medium-sized, slender Heron, slaty-blue, with a maroon-colored head and neck; legs dark.

The adult, like the Green Heron, appears quite blackish at a distance, but the latter bird is smaller, with much shorter, *yellow* legs.

The immature bird is snowy white with a tinge of blue in the primaries; legs dull greenish; bill bluish tipped with black. White birds changing to adulthood are boldly pied or spotted with blue, quite unlike any plumage of any other Heron.

GREEN HERON. *Butorides virescens virescens.*

A small dark Heron with comparatively short *yellow or orange* legs. Elevates a shaggy crest when alarmed. Looks quite black and Crow-like at a distance, but flies with slower, more arched, wing-beats.

Normally, this is the most generally distributed small Heron in the North.

BLACK-CROWNED NIGHT HERON. *Nycticorax nycticorax hoactli.*

A chunky, rather short-legged Heron. The adult is the only Heron that is black-backed and white below. Wings gray.

The immature is brown, spotted and streaked with white. It resembles the American Bittern, but is a grayer brown, rather than a rich, warm brown. In flight, it flaps its wings more slowly and lacks the broad black wing-tips of the Bittern. Its call, a flat *quok*, is unmistakable.

YELLOW-CROWNED NIGHT HERON. *Nyctanassa violacea.*

A chunky gray Heron with a black head; without the contrast of black above and white below of the Black-crown.

The immature is very similar to the young Black-crown, but is darker, the bill is slightly stouter, the legs yellower, and, in flight, the entire foot and a short space of bare leg extends clear of the end of the tail — a very good field character that is not shared with the Black-crown. The Yellow-crowned Night Heron is very different from the Black-crowned in flight. The flight is more suggestive of that of the Great Blue Heron.

AMERICAN BITTERN. *Botaurus lentiginosus.*

In crossing a marsh we frequently flush this stocky brown bird. Seldom do we notice it before it takes wing, and even more seldom do we see it perching in the manner of other Herons. The bold *black* wing-tips, contrasting with the yellowish brown of the rest of the bird, is a point that surely separates it from the similarly colored young Night Heron. When silhouetted in flight, so that color does not register, the faster wing-beats and the more curved wings are the Bittern's marks. Contrary to many a person's preconceived idea, the Least Bittern resembles it but little. It is much less than half the size and is contrastingly patterned with buff and black.

The pumping, the 'song' of the Bittern, which we hear in the swamps in the spring might be rendered thus: *oong-ka-choonk — oong-ka-choonk — oong-ka-choonk*, etc. Distorted by distance, the *ka* is often the only audible syllable and sounds like the driving of a stake into the bog.

LEAST BITTERN. *Ixobrychus exilis exilis.*

The Least Bittern is by far the smallest of the Heron family, hardly larger than a Rail, or about twelve inches in length. When discovered, it usually flushes close at hand from the reeds in which it has been hiding, flies weakly for a short distance, and drops in again. The *large buff wing-patches* and black back will distinguish it at once from any of the Rail family, which are quite uniform in coloration.

The call, a soft *coo-coo-coo* coming from the reeds, is often the best indication of the bird's presence.

CORY'S LEAST BITTERN.

A rare local color-phase of the Least Bittern. Identical in pattern with the Least Bittern, but having the buff color of that bird replaced by deep chestnut.

WOOD IBISES: CICONIIDÆ

Wood Ibis. *Mycteria americana.*

A very large white Heron-like bird with a dark, naked head and black wing-tips; bill long, stout, and decurved. Distinguished in flight, at a distance, from the white Herons by the outstretched neck and the black in the wings and by the alternate flapping and sailing; from the similarly patterned White Ibis by its entirely dark head, stouter bill, and much larger size (near that of the Great Blue Heron). (See cut, page 17.)

Young birds are dark gray with a downy covering on the head and neck.

IBISES AND SPOONBILLS: THRESKIORNITHIDÆ

Ibises are long-legged Heron-like birds with long, slender, *decurved* bills, similar to those of the Curlews. Unlike the Herons they fly with necks *outstretched.*

The name alone describes the Spoonbills. No other Heron-like birds have bills at all resembling theirs.

Glossy Ibis. *Plegadis falcinellus falcinellus.*

A medium-sized Heron-like bird with a long, decurved bill; largely bronzy-chestnut, but at a distance appearing quite black, like a large black Curlew. It flies with quicker wing-beats than a Heron, with neck outstretched, and feeds more like a shore-bird, pecking about in the mud.

White-faced Glossy Ibis. *Plegadis guarauna.*

Similar to the preceding species, but with a white patch about the base of the bill.

White Ibis. *Guara alba.*

Few sights in the bird world are as impressive as a large flock of these white birds drifting about in a great circle high in the air over some Southern marsh. Seen close at hand, they are medium-sized white Heron-like birds with black wing-tips, *red faces,* and long, decurved bills. They fly with necks outstretched, alternately flapping and sailing. No white Heron has black wing-feathers; the Wood Ibis has, but that bird is so very much larger that further comparison is hardly necessary.

a. WOOD IBIS   *b.* WHITE IBIS   *c.* GLOSSY IBIS

The brown young birds are quite evidently Ibises by their shape; the similarly sized young Glossy Ibis is uniformly dark, whereas the young White Ibis has white under parts.

SCARLET IBIS. *Guara rubra.*

A small bright-scarlet Ibis, of very rare occurrence along the Gulf Coast.

ROSEATE SPOONBILL. *Ajaia ajaja.*

A bright-pink Heron-like bird with a flat spoon-shaped bill. When feeding in the mud the flat bill is swung from side to side. In flight the neck is extended like an Ibis, but the bird does not sail between wing-strokes as habitually.

Three pink or red Heron-like birds may occur in the South — the present species, the Scarlet Ibis, and the Flamingo — but they are all so vastly different in shape that they could hardly be confused. The other two are extremely casual in our area; even the Spoonbill is rare enough.

FLAMINGOES: PHŒNICOPTERIDÆ

FLAMINGO. *Phœnicopterus ruber.*

An extremely slender rose-pink wading bird, with a broken 'Roman nose'; as tall as a Great Blue Heron, but much more slender. In flight its extremely long neck is extended droopily in front and its long legs trail droopily behind, as if the bird had scarcely enough strength to keep them up.

SWANS: CYGNINÆ

Very large white water-birds, larger and with much longer necks than Geese. Like some of the Geese, they migrate in stringy lines or V-shaped flocks. Their extremely long, slender necks and the lack of black wing-tips distinguish them from all other large white swimming birds (Snow Goose, White Pelican, etc.). Young birds are tinged with brown.

MUTE SWAN. *Sthenelides olor.*

In many parts of the East any wild Swan can be called, without hesitation, a Whistling Swan, but not so on Long Island, the New Jersey coast, and the lower Hudson valley. The Mute Swan, the park variety, has now established itself in numbers in a wild state throughout that area. It is in some respects a more graceful-looking bird than the somewhat smaller Whistler, nearly always swimming with a curve in its neck, and its tubercled orange bill pointing slightly downward toward the water. The Whistler at attention is quite stiff-necked, its head and bill jutting out at a right angle. It also

CANADA GOOSE

BRANT

BLACK BRANT

WHITE-FRONTED
GOOSE

ADULT   BLUE GOOSE   IMMATURE

SNOW
GOOSE

MUTE SWAN   WHISTLING SWAN

tends to sit lower in the water with less stern visible. When both species are feeding together, it will be observed that the Whistler works with its head and neck beneath the surface of the water a good deal more than does the other.

The young Mute Swan has a blackish bill, but the knob at its base is always a give-away.

WHISTLING SWAN. *Cygnus columbianus.*

The common wild Swan of the East. The cooing or honking of the birds can usually be heard long before the wavering wedge-shaped flock can be detected high in the blue. The much more stream-lined necks, and the lack of black wing-tips, eliminate the Snow Goose. Young birds are not white, but quite dingy-appearing.

The years of protection which have been theirs have made the Swans absurdly tame in many places; one can sometimes approach close enough to see the oval yellow spot at the base of the black bill.

GEESE: ANSERINÆ

Large waterfowl; larger, heavier-bodied, and with longer necks than Ducks. In flight some species assemble in V-formation. As is not the case with the Ducks, the sexes are alike at all seasons.

CANADA GOOSE. *Branta canadensis canadensis.*

Few people are unfamiliar with the long strings of these Geese passing high overhead in V-formation. Their musical honking, or barking, often heralds the approach of a flock long before it can be seen.

The Canada Goose, the largest and most common of its tribe in eastern North America, is a brownish bird with a black head and neck that contrast strikingly with the light-colored breast. Its most characteristic mark is the white patch that runs from under the chin on to the side of the head.

HUTCHINS'S GOOSE. *Branta canadensis hutchinsi.*

Almost identical with the Canada Goose, but smaller and with a shorter neck; not safely separable in the field.

AMERICAN BRANT. *Branta bernicla hrota.*

A small Goose, half the size of the Canada. It is chiefly coastal, bunching in large, irregular flocks rather than in the V-formation of most other Geese.

The Brant resembles the Canada Goose somewhat, but has a black head, neck, and breast, contrasting with a light belly, instead of a black head and neck contrasting with a light breast. In other words, the fore parts of a Brant are black to the water-line; a Goose's breast flashes white above the water. The Brant has a small white patch on the neck instead of a large white patch on the face. Then, too, as with all smaller birds, its wing-beats are less slow and labored.

BLACK BRANT. *Branta nigricans.*

A Pacific Coast bird, accidental on the Atlantic.

Similar to the American Brant, but with the under parts blackish to the under tail-coverts instead of showing the sharp contrast of black breast and light belly.

BARNACLE GOOSE. *Branta leucopsis..*

A European species that occasionally occurs on American shores.

Largely black and white with a *white face and forehead,* and a black mark extending from the eye to the bill.

WHITE-FRONTED GOOSE. *Anser albifrons.*

Smaller than the Canada Goose; near the size of the Brant.

The White-fronted Goose at a distance is a gray-brown bird and shows no contrast of black neck and light breast as in the Canada, or black breast and light belly as in the Brant. When flying overhead with either of those two species, the more uniform color below is at once apparent. At closer range the adult shows a clear white patch on the front of the face, black marks on the belly, and yellow feet. The young bird is uniformly dusky with yellow feet.

LESSER SNOW GOOSE. *Chen hyperborea hyperborea.*

A white Goose, smaller than the Canada, with *black wing-tips.* Swans are much larger, have longer necks, and lack the black wing-tips.

Young birds are duskier, but still white enough to be recognizable as Snow Geese.

GREATER SNOW GOOSE. *Chen hyperborea atlantica.* Like the Snow Goose, but averaging larger; the two are not separable in the field.

BLUE GOOSE. *Chen cœrulescens.*

A dusky Goose, smaller than the Canada, with a *white* head.

The young bird is uniformly dusky in color, very similar to the immature White-fronted Goose, but has pink legs instead of yellow as in that species, and paler, bluish wings.

SURFACE–FEEDING DUCKS: ANATINÆ

Ducks of this group, although not necessarily confined to small bodies of water, are most characteristic of creeks, ponds, and marshes. They obtain their food by dabbing and tipping up rather than by diving. When frightened, they spring directly into the air instead of pattering over the surface before getting under way. They swim with the tail held quite clear of the water; most Bay Ducks rest their tails flat on the surface. Most birds of this group have a metallic *speculum*, or ' *mirror*,' a rectangular patch situated at the hind edge of the wing.

MALLARD. *Anas platyrhynchos platyrhynchos.*

Male: — The male is distinctive, similar to, but smaller than, the domesticated Mallard of the barnyard; grayish with a green head, a narrow white ring around the neck, a ruddy breast, and a white tail. A few other Ducks have heads glossed with greenish and are, because of that, frequently mistaken for Mallards, but the white ring around the neck, and the ruddy breast, are diagnostic.

Female: — A mottled brown Duck with a whitish tail and conspicuous white borders on each side of the metallic wing-patch. Stray female birds, when mixed in with flocks of Blacks, appear much lighter in color, with a whitish tail. This and the white borders on the speculum are definitive field marks.

In sustained flight Mallards and Blacks have a characteristic wing-stroke; it is slower than in most Ducks, and the downward sweep does not carry the wings much below the level of the body. In bad light it is quite easy to confuse the two, but under normal conditions the striking pattern of the Mallard is quite evident.

COMMON BLACK DUCK. *Anas rubripes tristis.*
Both sexes: — Dark sooty brown with a lighter yellowish-brown head; feet brown or dull red; bill dull greenish; metallic blue patch on the wing; under surface of the wing silvery white.

The Black Duck in flight, with its uniform dark coloration and flashing white wing-linings, is unmistakable.

RED-LEGGED BLACK DUCK. *Anas rubripes rubripes.*
Males of the Red-leg, the Black Duck that comes into the States during the winter months, may be readily distinguished from the common Black Duck, even at a considerable distance, by its yellowish bill and bright red legs, and, if in company with other Black Ducks, by its larger size and paler-colored head. Another mark, perhaps the best one of them all, is the light-colored area on the wings near the back. The common Black has a trace of this, but it is not nearly so conspicuous. In dim light this is the most evident field difference.

The Red-leg can be identified with certainty as such only when in the plumage of the adult male.

FLORIDA DUCK. *Anas fulvigula fulvigula.*
The resident Black Duck of Florida. Similar to the common Black Duck but lacking the streaks on the throat. The light buffy of the throat contrasted with the darker color of the rest of the head is a good field mark.

MOTTLED DUCK. *Anas fulvigula maculosa.*
A darker race of the Florida Black Duck, found in Louisiana along the Gulf Coast and the lower Mississippi.

GADWALL. *Chaulelasmus streperus.*
A slender gray Duck with a white belly and a white patch on the *hind* edge of the wing.

BLACK DUCK

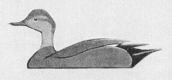

GADWALL · MALE

MALLARD

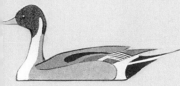

PINTAIL

WINTER   OLD-SQUAW   SUMMER
MALES

HARLEQUIN DUCK

RUDDY DUCK

Male: — Resembles the Black Duck, but is smaller, grayer, and more slender, and has a white belly. The white speculum is diagnostic. On the water the gray feathers of the flanks often conceal the white patch; then the best mark is the black tail-coverts, which contrast sharply with the general gray tone of the rest of the bird.

The head and neck of the Gadwall are thinner and snakier in appearance than those of any other River Duck except the Pintail. In the air it beats its narrow, pointed wings rapidly, in a manner quite different from that of the bulkier Black Duck.

Female: — Similar to the male but browner; resembles in shape and general color the female Pintail, but has a white speculum. It is quite likely to be confused with the female Baldpate, but that bird is more ruddy-colored, with a blue bill. The location of the white wing-patch is the best mark; that of the Baldpate is on the fore edge of the wing. Some females and young Baldpates in the fall show so little white in the wing that they might be easily confused with the Gadwall on this score.

EUROPEAN WIDGEON. *Mareca penelope.*
This European bird is not so scarce in the eastern United States as was formerly supposed.

Male: — Similar to the following species, but it is a *gray* Widgeon with a *reddish-brown head* and a buffy crown, instead of a brown Widgeon with a gray head and a white crown. It suggests, upon first acquaintance, a Redhead Duck. In bad light, or when too distant to show color, the head appears much darker than the rest of the bird, quite unlike the Baldpate, and the sides are much lighter with less contrast with rear white patch.

Female: — Very similar to the female Baldpate, but in very typical individuals under favorable light conditions it will be noted that the head is distinctly tinged with reddish, whereas that of the Baldpate is gray. The surest point, but one that can be noted only when the bird is in the hand, or very rarely in the field when the bird flaps its wings, is the appearance of the axillaries — dusky in this species, white in the Baldpate.

BALDPATE. *Mareca americana.*

The shining white crown of the male, which gives it its name, is the character by which most beginners learn this bird.

Male: — Mainly brownish in color with a gray head and a white crown; patch on the side of the head glossy green, visible only in good light; patch on fore part of wing white; bill blue with a black tip.

Female: — A ruddy brown Duck with a gray head and neck; belly and fore part of wing white.

The Baldpate in flight can be recognized at a good distance by the large white patch on the *fore edge* of the wing; in other Ducks possessing white patches they are placed on the hind edge. The similarly placed blue wing-patches of the Blue-winged Teal and the Shoveller often appear whitish at a distance, however.

Immature birds that have not acquired the white wing-patch are more nondescript. They may be best described as brownish Ducks with a paler gray head and neck, and a white belly which contrasts sharply with the brown breast.

PINTAIL. *Dafila acuta tzitzihoa.*

Pintails in flight are white-bellied Ducks with long, slim necks and long, *pointed* tails, quite different in cut and appearance from the other surface-feeding Ducks.

Male: — A slender gray and white Duck, characterized by the long, pointed central tail-feathers and a conspicuous white line running up the side of the neck and head. The light edgings of the rear of the Pintail's wings in flight is also a good character.

Female: — A slender, streaked brown Duck, similar to the female Mallard, but more slender and without the white-bordered blue speculum in the wing.

GREEN-WINGED TEAL. *Nettion carolinense.*

Male: — A small gray Duck with a brown head and a conspicuous *white mark* in front of the wing. In sunlight, the bird shows an iridescent green speculum in the wing and a green patch on the side of the head.

Female: — A little speckled Duck with an iridescent green speculum and no white in the wing.

BALDPATE

UROPEAN WIDGEON
MALE

CINNAMON TEAL
MALE

REEN-WINGED TEAL
MALE

EUROPEAN TEAL
MALE

BLUE-WINGED TEAL

SHOVELLER

WOOD DUCK

When Ducks fly up from pond-holes in a marsh, Teal are at
once conspicuous by their half-size proportions. If they show
two light-colored patches on the wings, then they are surely
this species.

EUROPEAN TEAL. *Nettion crecca.*
Extremely rare in North America. The male is very similar
to the male Green-winged Teal, but lacks the vertical white
mark in front of the wing, and has, unlike the Green-wing, a
horizontal white bar on the scapulars, *above* the wing.

BLUE-WINGED TEAL. *Querquedula discors.*
Male: — A small dull-colored Duck with a large white
crescent in front of the eye, and a large chalky-blue patch on
the fore edge of the wing. The blue, at a distance in some
lights, looks whitish.
Female: — Mottled, with a large blue patch on the fore
part of the wing.
Little half-sized marsh Ducks with large light-colored
patches on the front of the wing can quite safely be called
this species. The somewhat larger Shoveller is similarly
marked, but can immediately be recognized by its tremendous
bill. The Blue-winged Teal's bill is long proportionally by
comparison with other small Ducks, but not nearly so long
as a Shoveller's.

CINNAMON TEAL. *Querquedula cyanoptera.*
Accidental in the East.
Male: — A small, cinnamon-red Duck with large chalky
blue patches on the front edges of the wings.
Female: — Almost identical with the female Blue-winged
Teal, but a bit rustier and more coarsely marked.

SHOVELLER. *Spatula clypeata.*
Male: — Handsomely colored; largely black and white;
belly and sides rufous-red; head blackish glossed with green;
breast white; pale blue patch on fore edge of wing.
Female: — Mottled brownish, with the large blue wing-
patch as in the male.
The Shoveller is a small Duck, somewhat larger than a

Teal; best identified in all plumages by its tremendous long
and flattened bill, which in flight gives the bird a long ap
pearance to the fore of the wings. On the water the bird sit
very squatty and low, with the bill pointed downward, pre
senting a distinctive appearance when once known. Whe
observed broadside on the water, or flying overhead, th
pattern of the Drake is totally unlike that of any other Duck
It consists of five alternating areas of light and dark, thus
dark, white, dark, white, dark.

Wood Duck. *Aix sponsa.*
Rightly named, the Wood Duck is a bird of the forestec
bottomlands and woodland streams. The male is the mos
highly colored North American Duck.
Male in winter and spring plumage: — Highly iridescent
Words fail in describing the bird; the pattern diagram ex
plains it much better.
Female: — Dark brown with lighter flanks, a white belly
a dark crested head, and a white area about the eye.
Male in eclipse plumage (summer): — Similar to the female
but with the white face-markings and red and white bill of
the spring male.
On the wing, the white belly of the Wood Duck contrasts
very strikingly with the dark back; this is not so evident in
the other white-bellied River Ducks. This, and the short
neck, the fairly long tail, and the angle at which the bill is
pointed downward, are all good aids in identification. The
call-note is a peeping *who-eek* or *jeee.*

DIVING DUCKS: NYROCINÆ

Although birds of this group are often called "Sea Ducks"
for convenience, many are found commonly on the lakes and
rivers of the interior; primarily, they are birds of the more
open bodies of water. They all dive for food, whereas the
Surface-feeding Ducks rarely dive. In taking wing, they
do not spring directly upward from the water, but find it
necessary to patter along the surface while getting under
way.

REDHEAD. *Nyroca americana.*

Male: — Mostly gray, with black upper and under tail-coverts, black neck and breast, red-brown head, and blue bill.

The male resembles the Canvas-back, but is much grayer; the Canvas-back is very white. The Redhead has a high, abrupt forehead and a blue bill, in contrast to the Canvas-back's long, sloping forehead and blackish bill. The comparative profiles of the two birds can be made out at fairly long range. Redheads flock in much the same formation as Canvas-backs, but are apt to shift about more in the flock. They are shorter and chunkier than that bird, much more like the Greater Scaup in general contour. The gray wing-stripe distinguishes the more uniformly colored Redhead from the contrastingly patterned Scaup.

Female: — A brownish Duck with a broad gray wing-stripe and a blue bill.

The female differs from the female Scaup in having a gray wing-stripe and an indistinct buffy area about the base of the bill, instead of a white wing-stripe and a well-defined white patch at the base of the bill. The only other female Ducks with broad gray wing-stripes are the Canvas-back and the Ring-neck. The Canvas-back is larger and paler, with the long profile; the Ring-neck is smaller, darker, and has a conspicuous white eye-ring and a ring on the bill.

RING-NECKED DUCK. *Nyroca collaris.*

A black-backed Scaup.

Male: — Head, fore parts, and back black; sides light gray with a conspicuous white mark in front of the wing; bill crossed by two white rings. In flight, the only black-backed Duck having a broad gray wing-stripe.

The name Ring-billed Duck would be much more appropriate, as an examination at very close range is necessary to be aware of the dull chestnut ring that encircles the neck. The bird's carriage, when swimming, is more that of a surface feeder, or River Duck, with its tail often held quite clear of the water. The only other Sea Duck that habitually carries its tail in this manner is the Old-squaw, although some of the others will do so occasionally, especially the Lesser Scaup and the American Scoter.

The rather triangular head-shape is distinctive in both sexes.

Female: — Brown, darkest on crown of head and back; wing-stripe gray; whitish area about base of bill; white eye-ring, and ring on bill; belly, white. Differs from female Scaup in possessing a gray wing-stripe, white eye-ring, and a ring on the bill; from female Redhead by its smaller size, darker back, and the conspicuous rings about the eye and on the bill. Females are a little difficult to tell from the Scaup which they so often associate with, but the males can be picked out at a great distance, as no other species of this distinctive genus has a black back.

CANVAS-BACK. *Nyroca valisineria.*

Male: — White, with a reddish head and neck, black breast, and blackish bill.

Female: — Grayish, with a suggestion of the red of the male bird on the head and neck.

The long, sloping profile will separate either sex from any of the other species which they superficially resemble. In flight, Canvas-backs string out in lines or in V-formation. The long head, neck, and bill give the bird a front-heavy appearance, as if the wings were set far back.

GREATER SCAUP DUCK. *Nyroca marila.*

Male: — This is the common bay Duck that at a distance on the water appears to be 'black at both ends and white in the middle.' The flanks and back are finely barred with gray, but at any distance those parts appear quite white. The bill is blue; hence the gunner's nickname, 'Blue-bill.'

At a great distance, on the water, drake Golden-eyes and Scaup look somewhat alike, but where the Golden-eye has only a black head, the Scaup is black to the water-line.

All members of the Scaup genus (*Nyroca*) and the Golden-eye, are high fliers. Most other Ducks fly low.

Female: — Brown, with broad white wing-stripe and a well-defined white area at the base of the bill.

The two Scaups are our only Ducks possessing a broad white wing-stripe. The length of this stripe can often be used to separate the two in the field; the white in the Lesser extends about halfway along the hind edge of the wing, while in the

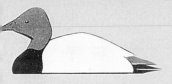

CANVASBACK

REDHEAD

RING-NECKED DUCK

GREATER SCAUP

LESSER SCAUP
MALE

GREATER SCAUP — LONG WHITE WING STRIPE
LESSER SCAUP — SHORT WHITE WING STRIPE

present species this stripe extends considerably farther toward the wing-tip (see diagram). This character does not always hold, as the birds sometimes intergrade, but typical individuals can be told in this way with a fair degree of certainty. Close at hand, in good sunlight, the black head of the Greater is glossed with green; that of the Lesser with dull purple.

LESSER SCAUP DUCK. *Nyroca affinis.*
Male: — Similar to the Scaup, but slightly smaller, comparatively larger-headed, and grayer on the flanks; head glossed with dull purple instead of green. These differences are slight and can be made out only when the bird is near-by in good light. The length of the wing-stripe is, when one has had a little practice, the easiest way to separate typical individuals in the field (see Scaup Duck).

The Greater is the winter Scaup of the Great Lakes and the northern Atlantic seacoast, while the Lesser, a less hardy species, is more of a fresh-water bird, the migrant Scaup that is so abundant on every lake and river in the interior.

GOLDEN-EYE. *Glaucionetta clangula americana.*
Male: — Largely white, with a black back and a black, green-glossed head. A large round white spot between the eye and the bill is the feature that sets this Duck apart from all the others. In flight the wings show large white patches.

The *male*, at a distance, bears a superficial resemblance to the male Merganser, but the Golden-eye is a stocky, very short-necked Duck with a large, round head, quite unlike the 'long-geared' Merganser. In many parts of the North, these are the two most typical winter Ducks.

Female: — Gray with a white collar and a dark-brown head; wings with large square white patches. The immature male resembles the female but lacks the white collar.

The mellow whistling sound produced by the Golden-eye's wings, which has earned for the bird the colloquial name 'Whistler,' is almost as good for identification as a sight of the bird itself.

BARROW'S GOLDEN-EYE. *Glaucionetta islandica.*
A northern species that winters uncommonly as far south as Massachusetts.

Male: — Similar to the drake Golden-eye, but with a greater amount of black on the sides of the body, a row of *white* spots on black scapulars, the black of the head glossed with purple instead of green, and a *crescent-shaped* white patch in front of the eye, instead of a round white spot.

Female: — The bill of the present species is quite yellow; otherwise the differences between the two species are too slight for use in the field.

BUFFLE-HEAD. *Charitonetta albeola.*

One of the smallest of our wild Ducks.

Male: — Mostly white, with a black back and a large, puffy black head marked with a great white patch that extends from the eye around the back of the head; large white wing-patches in flight.

Because of the large triangular white area on the head, it is sometimes mistaken for the Hooded Merganser, which is a very dark Duck instead of very white.

Female: — A dark little Duck with a large head, a white cheek-spot, and a white wing-patch.

OLD-SQUAW. *Clangula hyemalis.*

The long, pointed central tail-feathers of the Old-squaw are different from those of any other Duck except the Pintail, which is a Duck of the marshes, ponds, and rivers, rather than a bird of the ocean and the larger lakes.

Male in winter: — Patchily patterned with dark brown and white. Head, neck, belly, and scapulars white; breast, back, and wings dusky brown; dark patch on side of head; bill banded with black and pink.

Male in summer: — Mostly dark with white flanks and belly, and a white patch surrounding the eye.

Female in winter: — Lacks the long, pointed tail-feathers of the male. Dark above and white below; head white with a black crown and cheek-spot.

Female in summer: — Similar but darker.

The Old-squaw is the only Sea Duck showing a large amount of white on the body that has unpatterned dark wings. In flight old-squaws present a pied appearance with dark, pointed wings that dip low with each beat. They bunch in irregular flocks rather than in long, stringy lines like the Scoters.

REDHEAD

GREATER SCAUP

RING NECKED DUCK

CANVASBACK

BUFFLEHEAD

AMERICAN GOLDEN EYE

OLD SQUAW WINTER

MALE

HARLEQUIN DUCK

RUDDY DUCK

MALE

AMERICAN EIDER

SURF SCOTER

AMERICAN SCOTER

WHITE WINGED SCOTER

EASTERN HARLEQUIN DUCK. *Histrionicus histrionicus histrionicus.*

The Eastern Harlequin is extremely hardy and winters mainly north of the United States, but a few of them may occasionally be seen about wave-washed rocks and ledges on the New England coast.

Male: — A rather small dark blue-gray Duck (blackish at a distance) marked with white patches and spots. No other Duck is at all like it. A glance at the diagram will explain the bird's appearance better than any verbal description. In flight it has the shape, short neck, and manner of a Golden-eye. It often associates with Golden-eyes, among which it stands out as a uniformly black bird.

Female: — A dusky brown Duck with two or three round white spots on the side of the head. It may be distinguished from the female Buffle-head — which has only one white spot on the side of the head — by the absence of white in the wing; from the female Scoters, which it also resembles, by its smaller size. In short, it is a duck with the pattern of a female Surf Scoter and the shape of a Buffle-head.

AMERICAN EIDER. *Somateria mollissima dresseri.*

The Eiders are among the most strictly maritime of all the Ducks, rarely occurring far away from the rocky northern coasts. They are large and heavily built, and their flight is sluggish and low over the water. The head is rather low-hung, and the birds often progress with alternate flapping and sailing. No other Duck flies like them.

Male: — The only Duck with a *black belly* and a *white back* (King Eider has a black back). Breast and fore part of wing white; head white with a black crown.

Female: — A large heavily *barred* brown Duck.

The female Eiders resemble female Scoters because of their similar chunky proportions, but are of a richer, warmer brown color. None of the female Scoters have the heavy black vermiculations or barrings. The females of the American and the King Eiders are quite difficult to tell apart, but it can be done. The bill of the American Eider is longer and gives the bird a more sloping profile. The female King Eider is more coarsely marked, especially on the fore part of the wing.

The head of the female American Eider is a dull hair-brown, that of the King a decidedly *rusty* brown. This difference holds in the immature birds as well.

NORTHERN EIDER. *Somateria mollissima borealis.*

The Northern Eider is but a straggler on the coast of the northern United States, and it would hardly be safe to attempt to distinguish it in the field from the American Eider, so closely do they correspond in plumage. The yellow bill of the male American Eider has a frontal process that is wide and rounded where it terminates in front of the eye; this same process ends in a narrow *point* in the northern variety.

KING EIDER. *Somateria spectabilis.*

Male: — A large, heavy Duck; back and belly black; wings black with large white patches; breast and fore parts whitish; top of head pearl-gray; cheeks tinged with greenish; bill and large frontal processes orange.

At a distance the fore parts of the bird appear white, the rear parts black. No other Duck gives this effect. On the water it looks a little like a Black-backed Gull. (American Eider has a white back.)

Female: — A large, chunky brown Duck, heavily barred with black (see discussion under female American Eider).

Immature male: — Among the few birds of this species that occur farther south than the normal winter range there seems to be an unusually large percentage of young males, perhaps urged by that same *wanderlust* that is so generally characteristic of adolescence. These appear dusky, with light breasts and dark chocolate-brown heads. They show no square white wing-patches as would the female Golden-eye Duck, a species which might possibly be mistaken for them.

AMERICAN SCOTER. *Oidemia americana.*

Male: — The male American Scoter is the only American Duck with *entirely* black plumage. This, and the bright yellow-orange base of the bill, are diagnostic.

Female: — Dusky brown, with light cheeks contrasting with a darker crown. Females of the other two Scoters have two distinct white patches on each side of the head. At a distance in flight, the female American Scoter shows more light color

WHITE WINGED SCOTER

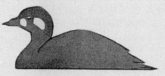

SURF SCOTER

AMERICAN SCOTER

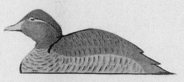

KING EIDER

AMERICAN EIDER
MALE

NORTHERN EIDER
MALE

on the under parts than the females of the other two species of Scoters.

WHITE-WINGED SCOTER. *Melanitta deglandi.*
The Scoters are the large, chunky, blackish Ducks that are commonly seen coastwise, flying in stringy formation low over the trough of the waves. The White-wing is the commonest and largest of the three species.
Male: — A black Duck with white wing-patches.
Female: — Dusky-brown with two white patches on the side of the head and a white wing-patch.

SURF SCOTER. *Melanitta perspicillata.*
Male: — Black, with two white patches on the crown of the head — hence the nickname of 'Skunk-head.'
Female: — Dusky-brown with two white patches on the side of the head. The smaller size and lack of a white wing-patch separate it from the similarly marked female White-wing.

RUDDY AND MASKED DUCKS: ERISMATURINÆ

RUDDY DUCK. *Erismatura jamaicensis rubida.*
Male in breeding plumage: — Largely rusty-red with *white cheeks*, black crown, and a large blue bill.
Male in winter: — Gray with white cheeks, a blackish crown, and a blue bill.
Female: — Similar to the winter male, but the light cheeks are crossed by a dark line.
In the air, in any plumage, the Ruddy appears as a small, chunky Duck, quite dark, and unpatterned in color except for the conspicuous white cheeks. The short wing-stroke gives the bird a very 'buzzy' flight. On the water it often cocks its tail vertically, like a Wren. It is possible to misidentify a female American Scoter as a Ruddy Duck — both are unpatterned except for light cheeks. Occasionally, the Scoter even cocks its tail. The Ruddy Duck is very much smaller with a definitely shovel-shaped blue bill.

MASKED DUCK. *Nomonyx dominicus.*
An occasional straggler from the Tropics. Smaller than any of our native species; somewhat like the Ruddy Duck.
Male: — Largely rusty with blackish stripes on the back, white wing-patches, and a black mask on the front of the face.
Female: — Like a small female Ruddy, but with *two* black stripes crossing each cheek instead of one.

MERGANSERS: MERGINÆ

Our three Mergansers, or fish-eating Ducks, lack the broad and flattened bills so characteristic of most of the Duck tribe; the mandibles are slender and narrow, equipped with toothed edges which are well adapted for seizing their slippery prey. Most species have crests and are long-geared, slender-bodied birds. In flight, the bill, head, neck, and body are held perfectly horizontal; at a distance, this gives them an unmistakable long-drawn appearance which is quite unlike that of any of the other Ducks.

HOODED MERGANSER. *Lophodytes cucullatus.*
Male: — Black and white, with a *fan-shaped white crest* on the head; breast white with two black bars in front of the wing; wing dark with a white patch; flanks brownish. The male, distinctive as it is, is often confused with the male Buffle-head. The Buffle-head is smaller, chubbier, and whiter; the flanks of the Buffle-head are white, whereas those of the Hooded Merganser are dark. The white head-patch of the Merganser is outlined with a narrow dark border.
Female: — Recognized as a Merganser when close at hand by the narrow, spikelike bill, and in flight by the long-drawn appearance of the bird, with bill, head, neck, and body held in a horizontal straight line. Differentiated from the other two female Mergansers by the small size, dark coloration, *dark head and neck*, and buffy crest. The female is sometimes mistaken for the female Wood Duck, which is also dark and has a crest, but the square white wing-patch and different flight will identify the Merganser.

AMERICAN MERGANSER. *Mergus merganser americanus.*
In line formation, low over the water, the American

AMERICAN MERGANSER

RED-BREASTED MERGANSER

HOODED MERGANSER

BUFFLEHEAD

GOLDENEYE

BARROWS GOLDENEYE
MALE

Mergansers follow with careful exactness the winding course of the creeks and rivers which they frequent. Like the others of the group, this species is a rakish, long-bodied bird. The large, white, black-headed males are unmistakable.

Male: — White, with a black back and a green-black head; bill and feet orange; breast tinged with a delicate peach-colored bloom. The whiteness of the bird and the Merganser shape, with bill, head, neck, and body all held perfectly horizontal, will identify it in flight a long way off. This species and the Golden-eye are the most typical winter Ducks over a great part of the northern United States away from the coast. They resemble each other superficially at a distance, but the Golden-eye, aside from having the conspicuous white spot in front of the eye, is a smaller, chubbier, shorter-necked, and rounder-headed bird.

Female: — Largely gray with a *crested* rufous-red head, orange bill and feet, and a large square white patch on the wing (see female Red-breasted Merganser).

RED-BREASTED MERGANSER. *Mergus serrator.*
Male: — Not so white as the American Merganser; black head glossed with green and *conspicuously crested*; area on the breast at the water-line brownish, whereas the same area in the American Merganser appears white; bill and feet orange.

Female: — Largely gray, with a crested rufous-red head and a large square white patch on the wing; bill and feet orange. Very similar to the female American Merganser, but the rufous of the head *blends* into the white of the throat and neck instead of being sharply defined as in that bird.

The Red-breasted Merganser is more characteristic of the ocean than is the American, which is more essentially a fresh-water species. Both birds may, however, at times be found on the same bodies of water.

VULTURES: CATHARTIDÆ

Vultures are great blackish Eagle-like birds, usually seen soaring in wide circles high in the heavens. Their naked heads are so small for the size of the bird that at a great distance they sometimes appear to be almost headless. Hawks and Eagles have large, well-proportioned heads.

Turkey Vulture. *Cathartes aura septentrionalis.*

This species, the better-known of the two eastern Vultures, is very nearly Eagle-size with great, ample 'two-toned' blackish wings (the flight feathers are noticeably lighter than the rest of the bird). It is usually to be seen high in the air, soaring on motionless wings in wide circles. The diminutive head and slimmer tail at once distinguish it from the Eagles. Of course, if the bird is close, a glimpse of the red color of the head at once clinches the identification. Young birds, however, have black heads and are sometimes mistaken for Black Vultures. A Turkey Vulture soars with its wings held perceptibly above the horizontal; an Eagle with its wings perfectly horizontal; and an Osprey with a decided kink, or crook, in its wings. Where all three are common this comparison helps.

Black Vulture. *Coragyps atratus atratus.*

One of the best points of difference between this black-headed species and the Turkey Vulture is the comparatively short tail which barely projects from the hind edge of the wings. So short is it that the extended feet stick out quite perceptibly beyond its tip. The tail of the Turkey Vulture is quite long and slim. A whitish patch toward the tip of the Black Vulture's wing on the under surface is also a sure mark. The wings are somewhat shorter than the Turkey Vulture's, and the bird flaps more frequently and soars less.

KITES: ELANINÆ

Hawks of southern distribution; most nearly resembling the Falcons in shape of wing — except the Everglade Kite.

White-tailed Kite. *Elanus leucurus majusculus.*

This species and the Mississippi Kite are Falcon-shaped, with long, pointed wings and a long tail, but the flight, although quite fast, lacks the dash of Falcons.

The adult is pale gray with a white head, *tail*, and under parts, and a *large black patch* toward the fore edge of the wing. No other Falcon-like bird (except the White Gyrfalcon) has a white tail.

The immature is similar but the tail is grayer.

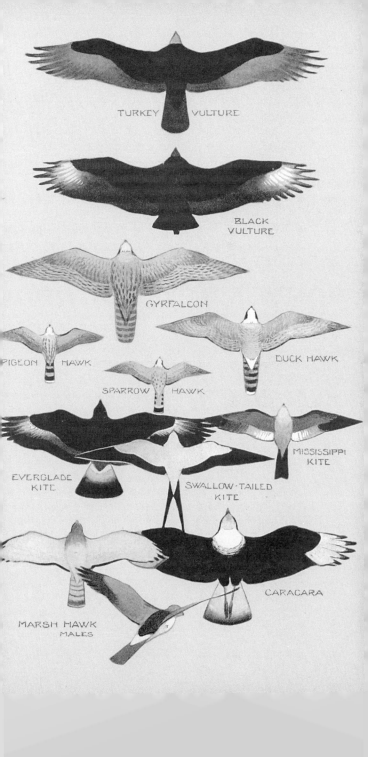

TURKEY VULTURE

BLACK VULTURE

GYRFALCON

PIGEON HAWK

SPARROW HAWK

DUCK HAWK

EVERGLADE KITE

SWALLOW-TAILED KITE

MISSISSIPPI KITE

MARSH HAWK MALES

CARACARA

SWALLOW-TAILED KITE. *Elanoides forficatus forficatus.*
Not only is this medium-sized Hawk shaped like a Barn
Swallow, but it even flies with similar grace. The black upper
parts, the white head and under parts, and the long, *forked*
tail, make it a striking, well-marked bird.

MISSISSIPPI KITE. *Ictinia misisipiensis.*
Falcon-shaped; gray, dark above and light below; head
very pale pearly gray; tail *black*. No other long-tailed Hawk
(except the dissimilar Swallow-tailed Kite) has a black tail.

EVERGLADE KITE. *Rostrhamus sociabilis plumbeus.*
Although grouped with the Kites, this species does not have
the Falcon-like shape of the others; the wings are more ample,
and the tail is wider. Adult males are black above and below;
females are light-bellied, with some white markings about the
head. The black plumage is rather rare. On the wing it
appears as a large black Hawk with a white area across the
base of the tail. The only other blackish Hawk native to
Florida with white at the base of the tail is the Caracara, which
would always show light wing-tips. The flight is a little like
that of a Marsh Hawk; the bird progresses leisurely, flapping
and sailing at a low height, until a snail is sighted, when it
checks its course suddenly and drops to seize it.

ACCIPITERS, OR SHORT–WINGED HAWKS: ACCIPITRINÆ

Long-tailed Hawks with short, rounded wings; woodland
birds that do not often soar about high in the air as do the
Buteos. The Goshawk is not properly an Accipter, but it belongs to this subfamily.

GOSHAWK. *Astur atricapillus.*
A large, long-tailed, short-winged Hawk with a pearly-gray
breast and a blue-gray back; of a lighter gray than any other
Raptor except the Marsh Hawk, which has longer wings. It is
easily told from the Cooper's Hawk, which it resembles in
shape, by its much larger size — considerably larger than
a Crow; Cooper's is smaller than a Crow. The gray-backed

adult Cooper's is reddish below; the Goshawk, gray. The lighter gray of the Goshawk's back is also distinctive.

Young accipitrine hawks are brown above and heavily streaked below. They all have much the same pattern. Size, although sometimes deceptive, is a reasonable point of difference between this species and the Cooper's. A well-pronounced light stripe over the eye in the young Goshawk is about the only definite point of distinction.

SHARP-SHINNED HAWK. *Accipiter velox.*
A small Hawk with a long tail and short, rounded wings. Size near that of Sparrow and Pigeon Hawks, but those two species have long, pointed wings. Large females are often near the size of small male Cooper's. The two are almost identical in pattern, but generally the Cooper's has a rounded tail and the Sharp-shin a *square-tipped* tail (slightly forked when folded).

COOPER'S HAWK. *Accipiter cooperi.*
A short-winged, long-tailed Hawk; not quite so large as a Crow. Keeps to the woods and does not habitually soar high in the open. Can be known from the Sharp-shin by its *rounded tail*, and from the Goshawk by its much smaller size.

BUTEOS, OR BUZZARD HAWKS: BUTEONINÆ
(*in part*)

Large Hawks with broad wings and broad, rounded tails, which habitually soar in wide circles, high in the air.

Black or melanistic phases often occur in birds of this group, especially in the Rough-legged Hawk. There is considerable variation in individuals within most of the species. This may cause a little confusion among beginners. Those that are figured in the pattern-diagram are in the most characteristic plumages. Young birds are similar to the adults, but are more or less *streaked lengthwise* below.

RED-TAILED HAWK. *Buteo borealis borealis.*
The tyro usually finds it necessary to wait till this large broad-winged, round-tailed Hawk veers in its soaring so that the upper side becomes visible. If the tail is not rufous-red, he

COOPER'S HAWK

GOSHAWK

SHARP-SHINNED HAWK

LIGHT PHASE

ROUGH-LEGGED HAWK

ABOVE

DARK PHASE

BROAD-WINGED HAWK

RED-SHOULDERED HAWK

RED-TAILED HAWK

SWAINSON'S HAWK

DARK PHASE

SHORT-TAILED HAWK

LIGHT PHASE

is then assured that the bird must be a Red-shoulder, but here he is often mistaken, for young Red-tailed Hawks do not have red tails. From beneath, however, adults have light tails with little or no apparent banding. Young birds may or may not show banding. The under parts of the Red-tail are more

IMMATURE RED-SHOULDERED HAWK

The Hawks shown in overhead flight in the plates are adults. Immature birds have the same shapes but in most instances are streaked below as in this bird.

or less zoned, that is, a broad band of dark streakings crosses the under parts midway. The Red-shoulder is uniformly colored below. With a good deal of practice one can easily identify the various Buteos by shape alone. The Red-tail is heavier, with wider wings and a shorter tail than the Red-shoulder's.

FLORIDA RED-TAILED HAWK. *Buteo borealis umbrinus.*

The resident Red-tail of southern Florida. A darker form than the preceding, with a broader black band (nearly an inch wide) at the tip of the tail.

KRIDER'S HAWK. *Buteo borealis krideri.*

Occasional in the Southeast in winter. In appearance, a partially albinistic Red-tail with much white mixed about in the plumage. The tail may range from pale red to white.

HARLAN'S HAWK. *Buteo borealis harlani.*

A *black* Red-tail with a *finely mottled* black and white tail. Occurs in the winter in the lower Mississippi valley.

RED-SHOULDERED HAWK. *Buteo lineatus lineatus.*

A common large Buteo, often seen circling on motionless wings high in the blue. Recognized as a Buteo by the ample tail and broad wings; distinguished from the Red-tail, which is chunkier, wider-winged, and shorter-tailed, by the banding across the under surface of the tail. The Broad-wing has a banded tail, too, but the bands are fewer and the white bands are as wide as the black. An infallible mark, shared by none of the others, is the light-colored spot toward the tip of the wings, at the base of the primaries. Nine times out of ten the diagnostic red shoulders of the adults are not visible; but close at hand, in good light, they are quite evident. The call of the Red-shoulder is a piercing *kee-you.* The Red-tail's cry is more like a squeal.

FLORIDA RED-SHOULDERED HAWK. *Buteo lineatus alleni.*

A smaller, whiter-headed form of the Red-shoulder, found from South Carolina, Alabama, and Oklahoma south.

INSULAR RED-SHOULDERED HAWK. *Buteo lineatus extimus.*

The Red-shoulder of the Florida Keys.

BROAD-WINGED HAWK. *Buteo platypterus platypterus.*

A rather small chunky Buteo, about the size of a Crow. The manner of banding on the tail is the best mark — *the white bands are about as wide as the black.*

Young birds are a little more difficult to tell, as the dark bands are more numerous, crowding out the white. The banded tail then resembles that of a Red-shoulder, but the bird is of distinctly different proportions, with a stubbier tail and shorter wings, more like a little Red-tail.

The call of the bird is ridiculously suggestive of that of a Wood Pewee.

SWAINSON'S HAWK. *Buteo swainsoni.*

Proportioned like a Red-tail, but the wings are more pointed. In the most characteristic phase the heavy dark breast-band is the best mark. The width of the band varies.

There are confusing lighter phases, where the breast-band nearly disappears, and black phases, but the bird is so very rare in the East that none but the commonest form as shown in the diagram should be recorded on sight evidence.

SHORT-TAILED HAWK. *Buteo brachyurus.*

A small Buteo, slightly larger than a Crow; found in the United States only in Florida.

Two color-phases occur — the 'Black Hawk' with black belly and black under wing-coverts, and the white phase, where the same areas are white. No other small Florida Buteo would be clear white or jet-black below.

AMERICAN ROUGH-LEGGED HAWK. *Buteo lagopus s. johannis.*

A Buteo by shape, but larger, with longer wings and a longer, more rounded tail than any of the others. As it often flies low in open country, it might easily be taken for a Marsh Hawk, especially because of the white base of the tail, but the Marsh Hawk is a slender bird, with a slim tail and long, slim wings. The Rough-leg is the only Buteo that *habitually* hovers, Kingfisher-like, or, like an Osprey, in one spot.

The normal, or light phase, from below, is distinguished by the well-defined black belly and the *conspicuous black patch at the wrist of the wing.* Light-bellied birds sometimes are seen. A black phase is quite common; all of these may readily be recognized by the striking under wing-pattern, with the large black patch at the wrist-joint.

FERRUGINOUS ROUGH-LEG. *Buteo regalis.*

A species of the Western prairies; casual east to Illinois.

Largest of all the Buteos; distinguished from the American Rough-leg by its coloration, ruddy above and whitish below, and the lack of a contrasting black terminal band on the whitish tail. A very good mark in typical light-bellied birds when flying overhead is a dark V formed by the dark chestnut-colored feathers of the legs.

HARRIS'S HAWK. *Parabuteo unicinctus harrisi.*
A black Buteo with a flashy white rump and a white band at the tip of the tail; like a Marsh Hawk in habits; occurs along the Gulf in Louisiana and Mississippi. The Harris's Hawk perched close to would show chestnut-colored areas — a mark of distinction from the melanistic Buteos (black Rough-leg, etc.).

EAGLES: BUTEONINÆ (*in part*)

Eagles are at once recognizable from the 'Buzzard Hawks,' or Buteos, which they somewhat resemble, by their immense size and proportionately longer wings. The powerful bill of an Eagle is nearly as long as the head, a point of distinct difference from the lesser Hawks.

GOLDEN EAGLE. *Aquila chrysaëtos canadensis.*
A Golden Eagle is a rare sight in the East, but undoubtedly they occur more often than the records indicate, as most bird-students are a bit uncertain as to what to look for. The light 'gold' on the hind neck is only occasionally of importance as a field mark. One does not often see Eagles close enough to distinguish such a mark.

The adult resembles the immature Bald Eagle. It may be evenly black below or it may show white at the base of the tail. When the bird wheels, showing the upper surface, the white tail, with its contrasting dark terminal band, identifies it. The amount of white varies. A young Bald Eagle going into adult plumage may have a tail that is whitish at the base, but never with a contrasting dark band. The present species has a more graceful, vulture-like flight, flapping less and soaring more than the Bald. Even the general contour is different; the wings are shorter and wider, the tail more ample. In brief, the bird is more Buteo-like, reminding one, not a little, of a Rough-legged Hawk. Perched at a distance, the bird appears flat-headed with a much smaller and less massive bill than the Bald Eagle.

BALD EAGLE   ADULT

BALD EAGLE   IMMATURE

GOLDEN EAGLE   ADULT

GOLDEN EAGLE   IMMATURE

OSPREY

Most Golden Eagles seen in the East are in the immature plumage, which is usually much more distinctive. From above or below, typical individuals show a *white flash in the wing* at the base of the primaries, and a white tail with a *broad, dark terminal band.*

All manner of variation exists between this 'typical' plumage of the immature and the plumage of the adult described above. The two extremes are shown in the plate.

BALD EAGLE. *Haliæetus leucocephalus.*
This, the typical Eagle of the East, needs little description. The adult, with its great size and *snowy-white* head and tail, resembles no other bird of prey.

The immature bird is dusky all over. Melanistic Buteos (black Rough-legs, etc.) are much smaller, with more or less gray and white under the wings. Some of the sight records of Golden Eagles in the East could doubtless be assigned to young birds of this species, although there are distinct points of difference that should render such mistakes inexcusable.

HARRIERS: CIRCINÆ

MARSH HAWK. *Circus hudsonius.*
The *white* rump-patch is the badge of the species. *Adult males* are pale gray; *females,* brown.

In ordinary flight the bird glides low over the meadows and marshes with the wings held perceptibly above the horizontal, in a manner suggestive of the Vultures. The white rump is always conspicuous. The Rough-leg has white at the base of the tail, but that bird is so heavily proportioned that it could hardly be confused with the slim Marsh Hawk. When the bird is flying high in the air, the long tail might suggest a Falcon, but the wings are not pointed. An Accipiter would have much shorter wings.

OSPREYS: PANDIONINÆ

OSPREY. *Pandion haliaëtus carolinensis.*
A large Eagle-like Hawk — blackish above and *clear white* below; the only really large bird of prey so patterned. The

head is largely white, suggestive of the Bald Eagle. Flies with a decided kink or crook in its wings. The Eagles and the lesser Hawks are all quite straight-winged. The habit of hovering, and plunging feet first for fish, is characteristic.

FALCONS: FALCONIDÆ

Hawks with long, *pointed* wings and long tails. The wing-strokes are rapid; the slim wings are not built for soaring in the manner of the Buteos. The Caracara, although vastly unlike the Falcons in appearance, is placed by systematists in this group because of similarities in anatomical structure.

AUDUBON'S CARACARA. *Polyborus cheriway auduboni.*
A large, long-legged, black Hawk, about the size of an Osprey; in the East found only in Florida. The under surface of the bird presents three alternating areas of light and dark — whitish throat and breast, black belly, and white, dark-tipped tail. In flight the *pale-colored patches* at the wing-tips are conspicuous from above or below. These are determinative, as no other bird of prey has anything quite similar.

WHITE GYRFALCON. *Falco rusticolus candicans.*
A very large Falcon, much larger than the Duck Hawk; the only Hawk that is really white. Distinguished from the Snowy Owl at a distance by the smaller head, pointed wings, and quicker flight. All Gyrfalcons are extremely rare in the United States.

BLACK GYRFALCON. *Falco rusticolus obsoletus.*
A large, blackish Falcon, much larger and blacker-breasted than the Duck Hawk.

GRAY GYRFALCON.
Since there are many intermediates between the Black and White Gyrfalcons, few definite marks can be cited. Only those that know the Duck Hawk from A to Z should attempt to recognize these rare birds. Aside from being very much larger, they are usually grayer and more uniformly colored, rather than contrastingly patterned with dark slate-color and whitish as is the Duck Hawk. The wing-beats are much slower.

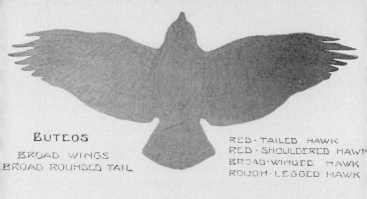

BUTEOS

BROAD WINGS
BROAD ROUNDED TAIL

RED-TAILED HAWK
RED-SHOULDERED HAWK
BROAD-WINGED HAWK
ROUGH-LEGGED HAWK

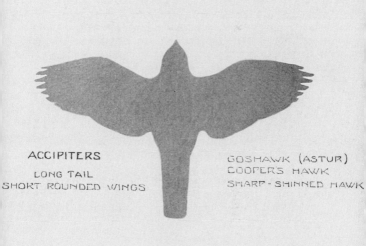

ACCIPITERS

LONG TAIL
SHORT ROUNDED WINGS

GOSHAWK (ASTUR)
COOPERS HAWK
SHARP-SHINNED HAWK

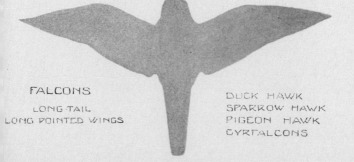

FALCONS

LONG TAIL
LONG POINTED WINGS

DUCK HAWK
SPARROW HAWK
PIGEON HAWK
GYRFALCONS

SILHOUETTES OF THREE COMMON TYPES OF HAWKS

DUCK HAWK. *Falco peregrinus anatum.*

The Duck Hawk is recognized as a Falcon by its long, pointed wings and long, narrow tail, and its *quick*, deep wing-beats that carry the wings far below the level of the body. Its size, near that of a Crow, identifies it as this species. The two other common Falcons, the Sparrow and Pigeon Hawks, are hardly larger than a Robin. On perching birds of this species the heavy dark 'moustachios' contrasting with the white cheeks are distinctive.

PRAIRIE FALCON. *Falco mexicanus.*

Casual east to Illinois. Very much like the Duck Hawk in size and appearance, but where the back of that bird is slaty-gray, almost blackish, this species is of a paler, sandy color. In flight overhead the Prairie Falcon shows large blackish patches (formed by the dark flanks and axillars) where the wings join the body. These patches contrast quite strikingly with the general light tone of the rest of the under surface.

PIGEON HAWK. *Falco columbarius.*

A small Falcon, hardly larger than a Robin. The male is bluish gray above, with broad bands on the tail. The female is browner.

The long, pointed wings and Falcon-like wing-action separate it from the little Sharp-shinned Hawk, which has rounded wings. The lack of any rufous red on the tail or upper plumage distinguishes it at once from the Sparrow Hawk. The flight is a bit different; the Pigeon Hawk cuts the air speedily, sailing less between strokes than the other bird. It also has a habit of frequently roosting on or near the ground.

During migration the Pigeon Hawk is looked for to best advantage in open country, coastal marshes, etc.

SPARROW HAWK. *Falco sparverius sparverius.*

A small Falcon, not much larger than a Robin. No other *small* Hawk has a rufous-red tail.

At a distance, in flight, the narrow, pointed wings eliminate the Sharp-shin, which has short, round wings. The usual flight, several strokes and a short sail, is rather distinct from the Pigeon Hawk's more swiftly cutting flight. Another good point to remember is that it is the only *small* Hawk that habitually hovers, Kingfisher-like, in one spot. The Sparrow Hawk, when perching, sits fairly erect with an occasional, but characteristic, jerk of the tail.

LITTLE SPARROW HAWK. *Falco sparverius paulus.*

The breeding Sparrow Hawk of Florida and the southern portions of the States bordering the Gulf.

GROUSE: TETRAONIDÆ

Ground-dwelling, Chicken-like birds that scratch for a living; larger than Quail, and without the long tails of Pheasants.

SPRUCE GROUSE. *Canachites canadensis.*

A dark dusky *slate-colored* Grouse of the deep, wet coniferous forests of the north country.

The male is splotched with black and white beneath. The female is browner, but always distinguishable from the Ruffed Grouse by the extreme duskiness of its plumage and the lack of a dark band near the end of the tail. At close range, such as only a Spruce Partridge would allow, the bird shows a patch of bare red skin about the eye.

RUFFED GROUSE. *Bonasa umbellus umbellus.*

A large, red-brown, Chicken-like bird of the leafy woodlands, usually not seen until it springs into the air with a startling whir. Female Pheasants are somewhat similar, but have pointed, instead of fan-shaped, tails, and usually prefer more open country. They flush with less of a whir, generally croaking as they go.

The drumming of the male bird is a sound that the beginner might overlook for a long time as a distant 'flivver' starting up on the other side of the woodland, or an outboard motor on some far-distant lake. The 'booming' starts off slowly, gaining speed until it ends in a whir: — *bup... bup... bup... bup..bup.bup.up.r.rrr.* At a distance the thumping is so hollow that sometimes it hardly registers as an exterior sound, but seems rather to be a disturbing series of vibrations within the ear itself.

CANADA RUFFED GROUSE. *Bonasa umbellus togata.*
The northern form of the Ruffed Grouse, which is found in the Canadian zone from central New York and northern Massachusetts north. Like the preceding, but with more gray and less rufous on the upper parts. The zone of intergradation is rather wide, both types often being found in the same woodland.

NOVA SCOTIA RUFFED GROUSE. *Bonasa umbellus thayeri.*
The Ruffed Grouse of Nova Scotia.

WILLOW PTARMIGAN. *Lagopus lagopus.*
Ptarmigan are small Arctic Grouse that change their brown summer plumage for white feathers when winter sets in. They frequent bleak, barren wastes and rocky slopes where few

PTARMIGANS IN WINTER
a. Rock *b.* Willow

other birds would long survive. Two species are found in eastern Canada, the Willow and the Rock Ptarmigan. They are very much alike; in the breeding plumage brown with white wings, and in the winter white with blackish tails. Perhaps there is no good way to tell the two apart in the field when they are in the brown plumage, but in winter the Rock Ptarmigan has a black mark extending from the bill through the eye. The smaller, more slender bill of the Rock Ptarmigan, the most constant feature, is apparent only when the bird is in the hand.

Any Ptarmigan occurring by accident within the eastern United States could be safely referred to the present species.

Two other forms of the Willow Ptarmigan occur: the Ungava Ptarmigan (*ungavus*), found in northern Quebec, and the Allen's Ptarmigan (*alleni*), the Willow Ptarmigan of Newfoundland.

ROCK PTARMIGAN. *Lagopus rupestris*. (See Willow Ptarmigan.)

The Rock Ptarmigan of Newfoundland has been named Welch's Ptarmigan (*welchi*).

PRAIRIE CHICKEN. *Tympanuchus cupido americanus*.

A large, brown Henlike bird of the brushy grasslands; known from the Ruffed Grouse by its open-country habitat, its very short, dark tail, and, if close, the heavy transverse barring on the under parts. The short, rounded tail distinguishes it from the point-tailed female Pheasants that might be found frequenting the same situations.

Found from Michigan and northern Ohio westward.

PRAIRIE SHARP-TAILED GROUSE. *Pediœcetes phasianellus campestris*.

A bird of the Western prairies that barely reaches the region covered in this book.

A *pale* Grouse with a *short pointed tail*. Female Pheasants have *long* pointed tails.

NORTHERN SHARP-TAILED GROUSE. *Pediœcetes phasianellus phasianellus*.

The form of the Sharp-tailed Grouse found to the north of the United States in the more open parts of the north woods. Much darker.

PARTRIDGES AND QUAILS: PERDICIDÆ

Small, scratching, Chicken-like birds, smaller than Grouse or Pheasants.

HUNGARIAN OR EUROPEAN PARTRIDGE. *Perdix perdix perdix*.

A grayish Partridge with chestnut-colored markings; smaller than a Ruffed Grouse and larger than a Bob-white; found in

RING-NECKED
PHEASANT
MALE

RING-NECKED
PHEASANT

FEMALE

RUFFED
GROUSE

PRAIRIE
CHICKEN

PRAIRIE
SHARP-TAILED
GROUSE

SPRUCE
GROUSE

BOB-WHITE

HUNGARIAN PARTRIDGE

WINTER

SUMMER

WILLOW
PTARMIGAN

farming country where it has been introduced. In flight the short, chestnut-colored tail is a good mark.

BOB-WHITE. *Colinus virginianus virginianus.*
A very small, ruddy, Chicken-like bird, much smaller than a Ruffed Grouse, or near the size of a Meadowlark. The clearly enunciated whistle *Bob White* is unmistakable. It is distinguished from the Ruffed Grouse by its smaller size and short tail; from the Woodcock, by its smaller head, stubby bill, and more blustering flight; and from the Meadowlark in flight by the lack of white outer tail-feathers.

FLORIDA BOB-WHITE. *Colinus virginianus floridanus.*
The peninsular Florida representative.

TEXAS BOB-WHITE. *Colinus virginianus texanus.*
The Texan variety has been introduced in many localities where the original form has been extirpated by gunning.

PHEASANTS: PHASIÁNIDÆ

RING-NECKED PHEASANT. *Phasianus colchicus torquatus.*
A large Chicken-like or Gamecock-like bird with a long, sweeping pointed tail. No other bird at all resembles it. The male is quite highly colored; the female is browner and more Grouse-like, but the pointed tail is always characteristic.

TURKEYS: MELEAGRIDÆ

EASTERN WILD TURKEY. *Meleagris gallopavo silvestris.*
The common domestic Turkey has white tips to the tail-feathers; the Eastern Wild Turkey, chestnut. This would be all well enough if it were not for the fact that the wild form sometimes breeds with stray runaway barnyard birds. As a result, it is quite difficult to determine the true identity of many individuals.

FLORIDA TURKEY. *Meleagris gallopavo osceola.*
The peninsular subspecies.

CRANES: GRUIDÆ

Cranes are long-legged, long-necked birds, superficially a little like large Herons. The most evident anatomical differences are the long feathers of the back, which curl down over the ends of the wings, the shorter bill, and the bare red skin about the face. Their blaring trumpet-like calls once heard will dispel any doubt as to their identity.

SANDHILL CRANE. *Grus canadensis tabida.*
A long-legged, long-necked, gray bird with a bald, red forehead.

The similarly sized Great Blue Herons are often called 'Cranes,' but the Heron in sustained flight carries its head drawn back to its shoulders, while the Crane flies with neck extended and legs trailing, like a 'flying cross.' (See cut, page 12.)

FLORIDA CRANE. *Grus canadensis pratensis.*
The Sandhill Crane of Florida and southern Georgia.

LIMPKINS: ARAMIDÆ

LIMPKIN. *Aramus pictus pictus.*
A large brown swamp wader of Florida and southern Georgia; about the size of a Bittern, but with much longer, *dark* legs, a longer neck, and a very long, slightly drooping bill. The bill gives the bird a slightly Ibis-like aspect, but no Ibis is brown with white spots and streakings. The flight is short and Rail-like, with the long legs dangling below.

RAILS, GALLINULES, AND COOTS: RALLIDÆ

Rails are somewhat Chicken-like marsh birds of secretive habits, shy rather than wary, and much more often heard than seen. When flushed, they rise from the reeds close at hand, fly feebly with legs dangling for a short distance, and drop back again suddenly into the marsh.

Gallinules and Coots resemble Ducks except for their smaller heads and rather Chicken-like bills.

KING RAIL. *Rallus elegans elegans.*
A large reddish Rail with a long, slender bill; twice the size of the Virginia Rail, or about that of a Chicken. The Virginia, the only other reddish Rail, has slaty-gray cheeks.

The call is a low, throaty *bup — bup — bup-bup-bup*, etc., much deeper and more vibrant than the corresponding call of the Virginia.

The King and the Clapper Rails are of similar proportions, but one is red, the other gray; the King inhabits fresh-water marshes; the Clapper, salt.

CLAPPER RAIL. *Rallus longirostris.*
This, the large gray Rail of the coastal marshes is the 'Salt-Water Marsh Hen' of the gunners. Its Henlike appearance, gray coloration, strong legs, and long bill will readily identify it. Its call, a clattering *cac-cac-cac-cac*, etc., is one of the most familiar sounds of the salt meadow.

The species has been split up into five subspecies in the East. As the points of distinction are slight, they are best identified by the locality in which they are found breeding:

EASTERN CLAPPER RAIL, *R. l. crepitans*, breeds from North Carolina to southern New England.

WAYNE'S CLAPPER RAIL, *R. l. waynei*, breeds from the lower corner of North Carolina to midway down the east coast of Florida.

FLORIDA CLAPPER RAIL, *R. l. scotti*, inhabits the west coast of Florida, and the lower east coast at Palm Beach and Jupiter Inlet.

MANGROVE CLAPPER RAIL, *R. l. insularum*, is the form found on the Florida Keys.

LOUISIANA CLAPPER RAIL, *R. l. saturatus*, is the Gulf Coast bird from Alabama to Texas.

VIRGINIA RAIL. *Rallus limicola limicola.*
A small reddish Rail, less than ten inches in length, with *gray cheeks* and a long, slightly decurved bill. It is the only small Rail, smaller than a Bob-white, with a long, slender bill.

Its most common calls are *cut-cutta-cutta*, etc., *wak-wak-wak*, etc., and *kidick-kidick*, besides various 'kicking' and grunting notes.

SORA. *Porzana carolina.*
The adult Sora is a small gray-brown Rail with a black patch on its face and throat, and a short, Chicken-like *yellow*

bill. This short yellow bill will distinguish the bird readily in any plumage from the only other similarly sized Rail of the cat-tail marshes it inhabits, the reddish Virginia Rail, which has a long, slender bill.

The 'song' of the Sora is a whinnying series of notes, quite unlike any performance of any of the others. In the spring a plaintive whistled *ker-wee* is characteristic. In the fall a sharp *keek* is the usual note of response when a stone is tossed into the marsh near them.

a. SORA   *b.* VIRGINIA RAIL

Showing the two types of bill existent in the Rail group

YELLOW RAIL. *Coturnicops noveboracensis.*

A small yellowish Rail, six or seven inches in length, showing a conspicuous *white* wing-patch in flight — the only Rail so marked.

Yellow Rails are so extremely secretive that it requires the services of a bird dog to hunt for them successfully. They prefer grassy marshes to the cat-tail swamps frequented by their larger relatives. The call is *kik, kik, kik, kik-ker-wey-er,* the latter three notes musical.

BLACK RAIL. *Creciscus jamaicensis stoddardi.*

A very tiny slaty or blackish Rail with a black bill; about the size of a young Song Sparrow with a bobbed tail.

All young Rails in the downy plumage are glossy black, and thus are often called Black Rails by the inexperienced. This species, like the Yellow Rail, inhabits wet grassy meadows and the margins of marshes, and is very difficult to flush. The *kick* notes are lighter and more metallic than those of the other Rails. More rarely the kicking 'song' ends in an unmistakable *croo-croo*.

CORNCRAKE. *Crex crex.*

A straggler from Europe that has occurred a few times on this side of the Atlantic.

A Rail of the short-billed Sora type, but nearly as large as a Clapper; largely *buffy* with large *rufous-red* patches on the wing-coverts.

PURPLE GALLINULE. *Ionornis martinica.*

Gallinules are Ducklike birds with stout, rather Chicken-like bills, equally at home swimming in the open water and wading in the shallows and among the reeds, or even perching in the bushes along the margin. The present species, which is one of the most beautiful of all water-birds, is especially typical of Southern swamps and rice-fields. In the North it is accidental.

The head and under parts are deep purple, the back glossy olive-green, the bill red tipped with yellow, frontal shield on the forehead light *blue*, legs *yellow*. Besides the more highly colored plumage, the *blue* frontal shield will separate it from the Florida Gallinule, and, in flight at a little distance, the bright *yellow* legs. It is more likely to be seen climbing about the bushes above the water than the other bird.

FLORIDA GALLINULE. *Gallinula chloropus cachinnans.*

A gray Ducklike bird with a red bill can, with certainty, be called this species. Outer under tail-coverts white.

Notwithstanding its name, this is the common Gallinule of the Northern States. The notes issuing from the marsh often have a whining quality, but are sometimes quite Chicken-like.

COOT. *Fulica americana.*

Largely gray with a blackish head and neck, white under tail-coverts, and a *whitish* Chicken-like bill. In flight a white border shows on the hind edge of the wing. It is the only slate-gray Ducklike bird with a whitish bill. Like the Gallinules, when swimming it pumps its neck and head back and forth to facilitate its progress. A Coot in the company of Gallinules is larger with a somewhat bigger head. As a rule it frequents more open bodies of water than the other bird. The dabbing motion, while feeding, is also quite characteristic. In deep water it dives expertly. When it takes wing, it patters its feet over the water for a considerable distance.

a. COOT   *b.* FLORIDA GALLINULE

OYSTER–CATCHERS: HÆMATOPODIDÆ

AMERICAN OYSTER-CATCHER. *Hæmatopus palliatus palliatus.*
A very large, flashy, dark and white shore-bird, about the size of a Crow, with a large *red* bill. It does not resemble, even remotely, any other Eastern bird.

PLOVERS AND TURNSTONES: CHARADRIIDÆ

Wading birds, more compactly built, more contrastingly patterned, and with shorter, stouter bills than Sandpipers.

LAPWING. *Vanellus vanellus.*
An accidental straggler from Europe.
A very large Plover, larger than either the Killdeer or the Black-belly; legs comparatively short; breast crossed by one very wide black band; tail ringed broadly with black and white; head with a long wisp-like crest. *No native shore-bird has a crest.*

PIPING PLOVER. *Charadrius melodus.*
A small, pale whitish Plover, with a more or less complete or incomplete black ring about the neck. The back of the little Semipalmated Plover is the color of wet sand; that of the Piping is more like the sun-bleached, dry sand of the shell-strewn beaches which it inhabits.
The common note is a plaintive, whistled *peep-lo.*

CUBAN SNOWY PLOVER. *Charadrius nivosus tenuirostris.*
A small Plover, slightly smaller and even whiter than the Piping Plover, from which it can be distinguished by its slim, black bill and *black legs* (Piping Plover, yellow legs). The ring in this species is reduced to a black patch on each side of the breast.

SEMIPALMATED PLOVER. *Charadrius semipalmatus.*
A small, ring-necked shore-bird, brown above and white below; half the size of the Killdeer, from which it may also be distinguished by the short tail and the *single* ring about the neck instead of two. The Piping Plover is similarly patterned, but is much paler and whiter.
The note is a plaintive *cher-we.*

WILSON'S PLOVER. *Pagolla wilsonia wilsonia.*
A ring-necked Plover, larger than either the Semipalmated or Piping Plover, from which it is easily distinguished by its *long, heavy, black bill.* The stubby little bills of the other two are black only at the tip. (See cut on next page.)
The notes of the various Plovers are so distinctly different that they can be used to advantage in learning the birds. That of the present species is a whistled *wheep!*

MOUNTAIN PLOVER. *Eupoda montana.*

Accidental in the East. Like a small Killdeer, but with no breast-rings. In the breeding season a black mark extends from the bill through the eye. In winter plumage the bird lacks this, but may be told from the winter Golden and Black-bellied Plovers, which it resembles somewhat, by the even coloration of its back, *devoid of mottling.*

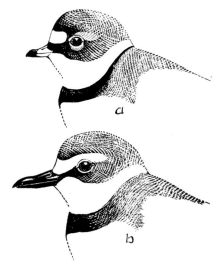

a. SEMIPALMATED PLOVER
b. WILSON'S PLOVER
Note the comparative bill-proportions

KILLDEER. *Oxyechus vociferus vociferus.*

The Killdeer is the common breeding Plover of the plowed fields and pasture-lands; the noisy shore-bird that reiterates its name so insistently as we trespass on its chosen ground. It is larger than most of the smaller Sandpipers and Plovers (about eleven inches), has *two* breast-bands, instead of one, as have all the other ringed Plovers, and, in flight, shows an ample, golden-red tail.

GOLDEN PLOVER. *Pluvialis dominica dominica.*

A medium-sized shore-bird, somewhat larger than a Killdeer.

Spring adults are brown above and black below, with a broad white line extending over the eye down the side of the head. The only other similar bird is the Black-bellied Plover, which is pale gray above, not golden-brown, and has a white rump and tail. The Golden Plover has a brown tail. When the two species are in the air together, the Goldens can be picked out readily by their more uniform coloration.

Young birds and winter adults are brown, darker above than below. They are recognized as Plovers, as distinct from Sandpipers, by their stocky proportions and short, stout bill; from the corresponding plumages of the Black-bellied Plover by the lack of white in the wings and tail, and the lack of black axillary feathers beneath the wings (where the wings join the body).

The harsh, whistled *queedle* or *quee* is quite unlike the plaintive *wheer-ee* of the Black-belly. The bird has other calls, some of them quite pleasing.

BLACK-BELLIED PLOVER. *Squatarola squatarola.*

In summer dress the Black-bellied Plover, with its black under parts, resembles no other shore-bird except the Golden Plover. The latter is a much browner-backed bird; the gray upper parts of the Black-belly appear quite whitish by contrast with the black breast.

Immature and winter birds are white-breasted and gray-backed; recognized as Plovers by their stocky proportions and short, stout bills.

In any plumage the *black* axillary feathers under the wing, and the white rump and tail, are determinative.

RUDDY TURNSTONE. *Arenaria interpres morinella.*

A squat, robust, orange-legged shore-bird, considerably larger than a Spotted Sandpiper. The adult in high breeding plumage with its russet-red back, white head and under parts, and the fantastic black face and breast markings, is handsome enough, but when the bird opens its wings in flight the real revelation occurs. This pied, harlequin pattern, which has given the Turnstone the nickname 'Calico-bird,' is best explained by the diagram. Young birds and winter adults are more sober in color, but the startling wing-pattern is quite constant.

WOODCOCK, SNIPE, SANDPIPERS, ETC.: SCOLOPACIDÆ

Small or medium-sized waders with more slender bills than Plovers. Most species are of plain or sober coloration.

Woodcock. *Philohela minor.*
A large, chunky, almost neckless, russet-colored bird, a little larger than a Bob-white (ten or twelve inches), with an extremely long bill. It resembles the Wilson's Snipe, but is usually flushed from a woodland swamp or leafy thicket, rather than an open, wet meadow, such as the Snipe chooses, and makes away on a straight course, often producing a whistling sound with its short, rounded wings as it flies. The snipe is slimmer, has *pointed* wings, and makes off in a zigzag fashion when flushed.

At night-time in the mating season the male emits a low nasal *peent*, a sound that suggests very much the call of the Nighthawk.

European Woodcock. *Scolopax rusticola rusticola.*
Accidental in eastern North America. Much larger than our native Woodcock and having the under parts *barred with black*.

Wilson's Snipe. *Capella delicata.*
A striped brown bird, larger than a Spotted Sandpiper, with a short orange tail and an extremely long, slender bill. When flushed, it makes off in a zigzag manner, uttering a sharp, rasping note (see Woodcock).

Long-billed Curlew. *Numenius americanus americanus.*
The Long-billed Curlew is now so very rare in the East that sight identification should be made with great care. Except in birds with extremely long-bills, bill-length is not always reliable, as some female Hudsonian Curlews have longer bills than some male Long-bills. The best points of distinction are

UPLAND PLOVER

BUFF - BREASTED SANDPIPER

HUDSONIAN CURLEW

HUDSONIAN GODWIT

MARBLED GODWIT

SOLITARY SANDPIPER

WILLET

FALL
SANDERLING

LESSER YELLOW-LEGS

FALL
NORTHERN PHALAROPE

OYSTER-CATCHER

STILT SANDPIPER FALL

FALL
RED PHALAROPE

TURNSTONE

WILSON'S PHALAROPE FALL

SHOREBIRDS I

the much larger size of the Long-bill, the more *buffy* coloration, and the lack of contrasting head-striping (i.e., dark line
through eye, light median line through crown, etc.). In flight,
overhead, the *bright cinnamon wing-linings* make the surest
identification mark.

HUDSONIAN CURLEW. *Phæopus hudsonicus.*
Curlews are very large brown shore-birds with long, *down-
curved* bills. The bills of Godwits turn up. In flight they
appear quite as large as some Ducks, and when in small flocks
often fly in line or wedge-formation, with sickle bills extended
and legs trailing. In the East this is the only common Curlew;
so it is quite safe to refer all sight records automatically to this
species.

ESKIMO CURLEW. *Phæopus borealis.*
The Eskimo Curlew is now very near extinction if not
extinct. There have been recent sight records.
The bird resembles the Hudsonian Curlew; is smaller, with
a shorter, stubbier bill (young Hudsonian Curlews have fairly
short bills), and lacks the well-defined light median stripe
through the center of the dark crown. The decisive mark is the
lack of broad barring on the long primary wing-feathers.
These feathers are *solid dark* in the Eskimo Curlew.

UPLAND PLOVER. *Bartramia longicauda.*
A large buffy-brown shore-bird, larger than a Killdeer but
with no really distinctive markings; inhabits high ground,
fields, burnt meadows, etc., refusing to accept the restricted
pastures in which Killdeer nest. It habitually resorts to fence-
posts and even telegraph-poles. The general brown coloration, the rather short bill, the comparatively short-legged,
long-necked, long-tailed appearance, and the habit of holding
the wings elevated upon alighting are all helpful points of
recognition.
The call is a very distinctive whistle, long drawn out and
melodious.

SPOTTED SANDPIPER. *Actitis macularia.*
Everyone knows this shore-bird. It is the common breeding

Sandpiper; the one that is found at some time or other on nearly every lake, pond, and stream the breadth of the country. It runs along the margin, teetering up and down between steps as if it were a little too delicately balanced on its slim legs.

In the breeding plumage the breast is covered with *large round spots* like those of a Wood Thrush; many Sandpipers are streaked, but this is the only one that is definitely spotted.

Juvenile birds and fall adults lack this distinctive spotting. They are olive-brown above and whitish below, with a white line over the eye. A white mark on the shoulder is a good aid in identification. The constant teetering is as good a characteristic as any, when the bird is on the ground. The wingstroke is very short, below the horizontal, the wings maintaining a stiff, bowed appearance, entirely unlike the more deep-sweeping flight of the other small shore-birds. With this distinction learned, it is hardly necessary to scrutinize further every Sandpiper of this species that rises from the margin, in the hope that it may be one of the less common varieties. A white wing-stripe, more broken than that of other small shore-birds having similar stripes, shows in flight. The call is a well-enunciated *peet-weet!* (See Solitary Sandpiper.)

SOLITARY SANDPIPER. *Tringa solitaria solitaria.*

A dark Sandpiper, blackish above and whitish below. A white eye-ring is a conspicuous mark. Resembles a little Yellow-legs, and nods like one, but has a black rump instead of white, and dark legs instead of yellow. A Spotted Sandpiper *teeters* more than it nods and has a white stripe in the wing, which the Solitary lacks; the Spotted has a narrow wing-arc; the Solitary, deep. Both frequent similar situations and both say *peet-weet*, but the call of the Solitary is higher-pitched.

In short, the Solitary may best be described as *a dark-winged Sandpiper with white sides to the tail, which are very conspicuous in flight.*

EASTERN WILLET. *Catoptrophorus semipalmatus semipalmatus.*

A large gray and white shore-bird, much larger than a Yellow-legs, with *flashy black and white wings*. The other really large shore-birds (except the dissimilar Oyster-catcher) have dark, unpatterned wings. At rest, when the banded wings cannot be seen, the bird is rather nondescript. It is Yellow-legs-like in appearance, large and slender, but with not so much contrast between the tones of the upper and under parts. The legs are bluish. The call is an oft-repeated *pill-will-willet!*

WESTERN WILLET. *Catoptrophorus semipalmatus inornatus.*
In the interior, and along the Atlantic Coast where the Eastern form does not breed, the Western Willet has been said to be the common migrant, especially in the fall. Actually, most of the specimens taken prove to be puzzling intermediates. At this season it is supposedly possible to identify the Western Willet in the field. It is said to be larger and paler-colored on the back, to have no streaking at all on the breast, and to have a noticeably longer bill.

In the South there are certain times during migration when both may be seen together on the same marsh-flats. Extremes are probably separable, but many individuals come so near to both types that no positive distinction can be made.

GREATER YELLOW-LEGS. *Totanus melanoleucus.*
A rather large, slim, gray and white sandpiper with *bright yellow legs*. Flying, it appears as a dark-winged shore-bird with a whitish rump and tail.

The three- or four-syllabled whistle, *whew-whew-whew*, is distinctive. Both Yellow-legs have a 'yodeling' call, that of this species is a fast-repeated *whee-oodle, whee-oodle*, etc.

LESSER YELLOW-LEGS. *Totanus flavipes.*
Exactly like the Greater Yellow-legs in color, but considerably smaller. The smaller, slimmer bill of the Lesser is perfectly straight; that of the Greater, *slightly upturned*.

The notes have a different ring; the call most often given by the Greater as it rises from the mud-flat is a clear, three-syllabled *whew-whew-whew*. The corresponding call of the Lesser is a flatter, less penetrating cry of one or two notes, *cu* or *cu-cu*. (See Stilt Sandpiper and Wilson's Phalarope.)

KNOT. *Calidris canutus rufus.*
Stout and chunky; larger than a Spotted Sandpiper.

In the spring the breast of the Knot is light Robin-red. The short bill, about as long as the head, will distinguish it from the Dowitcher, which is also red-breasted at this season.

In the fall the bird is more nondescript, the red of the breast being replaced by white. The general appearance is that of a dumpy light-grayish shore-bird with short legs, a short bill, and a whitish rump. In flight the whitish rump does not show so conspicuously as that of the Yellow-legs, nor does it extend so far up the back as in the Dowitcher.

PURPLE SANDPIPER. *Arquatella maritima.*

Flocks of Sandpipers seen flying about rocky, wave-washed isleus off the northern coast in winter can safely be assigned to this species — a hardier bird than the rest of the kin. It seldom occurs south of New England.

The rock-feeding habits, stocky build, and rather Junco-like coloration, with slate-gray back and breast and white belly, are good field marks. It may often be approached close enough to make out the short yellow or orange legs and the yellow base of the bill.

PECTORAL SANDPIPER. *Pisobia melanotos.*

A streaked, brown Sandpiper, larger than a Spotted; prefers grassy mud-flats and short-grass marshes. The brown back is streaked with rusty and lined with white. The most characteristic thing about the bird is the heavily streaked breast, which is defined sharply against the white belly. In courtship the streaked chest is puffed out; hence, the appellation 'Pectoral.' The Least Sandpiper is colored similarly, but is but half the size. The top of the head is darker and the neck longer than that of any of the other shore-birds with which it might be confused. There is a good deal of size-variation in the Pectoral Sandpiper. Small individuals are likely to be confused with the following two species.

WHITE-RUMPED SANDPIPER. *Pisobia fuscicollis.*

The only small streaked Sandpiper with a *white* rump; most of the others have white or whitish sides to the tail, but none possesses the white basal patch of this species. It is larger than the Semipalmated Sandpiper and smaller than the

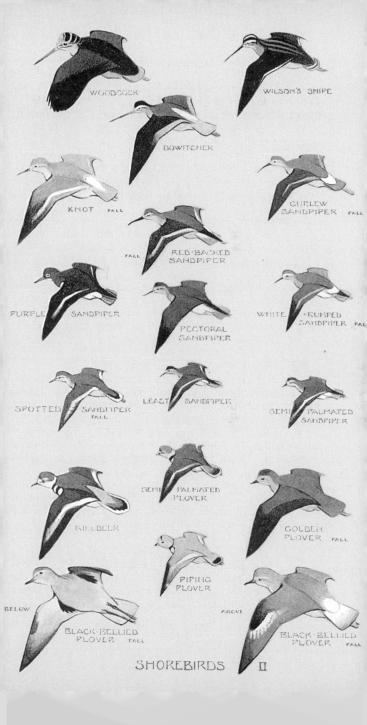

WOODCOCK

WILSON'S SNIPE

DOWITCHER

KNOT   FALL

CURLEW
SANDPIPER   FALL

FALL   RED-BACKED
SANDPIPER

PURPLE   SANDPIPER

PECTORAL
SANDPIPER

WHITE · RUMPED
SANDPIPER   FALL

SPOTTED   SANDPIPER
FALL

LEAST   SANDPIPER

SEMI · PALMATED
SANDPIPER

SEMI · PALMATED
PLOVER

KILLDEER

GOLDEN
PLOVER   FALL

BELOW

PIPING
PLOVER

ABOVE

BLACK-BELLIED
PLOVER   FALL

BLACK-BELLIED
PLOVER   FALL

SHOREBIRDS   II

Pectoral, or about the size of a Spotted. In the spring it is quite rusty; in the fall, gray, grayer than any of the rest of those which it resembles. The similarly sized Baird's Sandpiper does not have the conspicuous back-stripings of this bird, and the spring Semipalmated always shows a narrow strip of white separating the dark of the wing from the dusky streaking of the breast. The grayness of the plumage is the best mark in the fall. The fall Red-back is somewhat similar but larger, with a much longer, more decurved bill. *If in doubt, flush the bird and look for the white rump.*

The note, a squeaky mouse-like *jeet*, is of similar quality to the *jee-jeet* note of the Pipit. It has been likened to the scraping of two flint pebbles — a note totally unlike that of any other shore-bird.

BAIRD'S SANDPIPER. *Pisobia bairdi.*

The rarest of the 'Peep' Sandpipers. Larger than the Semipalmated and smaller than the Pectoral. Resembles a large Least or Semipalmated Sandpiper, but has a *very buffy head and breast*. Those two smaller species, the similarly sized White-rump, and the larger Pectoral are more or less *striped* on the back; the Baird's has a more *scaly* appearance, and the predominating color is buff. The Buff-breasted Sandpiper is buffy from throat to under tail-coverts, not on breast alone, and has yellowish, not blackish, legs.

LEAST SANDPIPER. *Pisobia minutilla.*

Collectively we call the small Sparrow-sized Sandpipers 'Peep.' These include the Least, Semipalmated, Western, Baird's, and White-rump. All of them have a characteristic streaked, brown pattern which, if we except the larger Pectoral Sandpiper, sets them, as a group, apart from the others. The Least is the smallest of them all. It may be known from the slightly larger Semipalmated Sandpiper by the *yellowish*, or *greenish*, instead of blackish or greenish-black, legs, the browner coloration, the *thinner* bill, and the more heavily streaked breast. (See cut on next page.)

The notes are reliable when once learned; that of the present species has more of an *ee* sound to it than that of the Semipalmated.

CURLEW SANDPIPER. *Erolia testacea.*

One of the rarest of shore-birds; characterized by the slim, down-curved, slightly Curlew-like bill.

In the breeding plumage it is reddish-breasted, a little like a spring Dowitcher, but the Dowitcher's bill is quite straight.

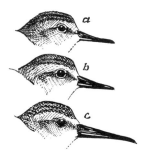

TYPICAL BILLS OF 'PEEP'
($\frac{5}{8}$ natural size)

a. Least Sandpiper   *b.* Semipalmated Sandpiper
c. Western Sandpiper

In winter plumage it very closely resembles the winter Red-backed Sandpiper, but is slenderer, longer-legged, and less streaked on the breast, and the bill is curved slightly throughout its length, not dropped only at the tip. All these things are differences of degree only; one must know the commoner bird extremely well to be sure of them. There is one definite point of distinction: the Curlew Sandpiper shows a *whitish rump* when it flies; the rump of the Red-back is whitish along the sides only. The white-rumped sandpiper is shorter-legged, shorter-billed and like the Red-back shows considerably more gray on the breast.

RED-BACKED SANDPIPER. *Pelidna alpina sakhalina.*

Slightly larger than a Spotted Sandpiper.

In spring plumage: — Rusty-red above, with a black patch across the belly and a white breast. No other *Sandpiper* has a black belly. (Black-bellied and Golden Plovers are black below.)

In winter plumage: — Plain, unpatterned gray above, with a gray suffusion across the breast; lighter than a Purple Sandpiper, much darker than a Sanderling. The best mark is the rather long stout bill for a bird of that size, which has a marked *downward droop* at the tip.

DOWITCHER. *Limnodromus griseus griseus.*

In any plumage this shore-bird can be recognized by its extremely long Snipe-like bill and *white* lower back, rump, and tail. The Wilson's Snipe, the only other bird with similar proportions, is rarely found on the beaches and flats where the Dowitcher feeds.

LONG-BILLED DOWITCHER. *Limnodromus griseus scolopaceus.*

The bill measurements of the two Dowitchers overlap, but extreme long-billed birds of this subspecies are easily recognized; the length of the bill, by comparison, dwarfs the head, giving the bird a small-headed appearance. There is also an indescribable, though very apparent, difference in the notes of the two birds. With the knowledge that there is such a difference, experience will help where description fails.

STILT SANDPIPER. *Micropalama himantopus.*

In autumn, the season when we are most likely to see it, the Stilt resembles a Lesser Yellow-legs, but is smaller, has a conspicuous white stripe over the eye, and has *greenish*, not yellow, legs. The bill, which is proportionately longer and heavier, tapering markedly and with a slight droop at the tip, is perhaps the most distinctive mark.

The Stilt usually feeds in deeper water than most shorebirds, often wading clear up to its belly. It slightly resembles the Dowitcher in certain respects and often is found in its company, but the whiter under parts, longer legs, and slimmer build distinguish it. In spring, when it is rare in the East, the bird is darker, heavily marked with *transverse* bars beneath.

SEMIPALMATED SANDPIPER. *Ereunetes pusillus.*

The only other common 'Peep,' or Sparrow-sized Sandpiper, is the **Least Sandpiper**. The shorter, *stouter* bill of the 'Semi' is the most constant point of distinction. (See cut, page 64.) The bird is noticeably larger, is grayer above, not so brown, and usually has *blackish*, instead of yellowish or dull green, legs. In the fall the streaky breast-band extends clear across in the Least Sandpiper, while that of the present species is reduced to a dusky patch on each side of the breast.

WESTERN SANDPIPER. *Ereunetes mauri*.

One of the most difficult of Sandpipers to identify in the field; when mixed in with Semipalmated Sandpipers, it appears a little larger and more coarsely marked. The bill is *very noticeably longer, and thicker at the base*. (See cut, page 64.) Young females have whiter heads.

In the breeding plumage it is much rustier on the back and crown than the Semipalmated. A trace of this rusty is often evident on the scapulars in the fall. In late summer or early fall the more complete band of breast-streaking is a good point. The breast-band of the commoner bird is reduced at that season to a dusky smudge at each side of the breast. The feet are black; hence there is no confusion with the Least Sandpiper, which might be more or less rusty on the upper parts.

The Western frequently forages about in deeper water than is usual with the other 'Peeps.'

BUFF-BREASTED SANDPIPER. *Tryngites subruficollis*.

A rather small, buffy shore-bird (slightly chunkier than the Spotted), with a short bill, round head, and yellowish legs; looks like a miniature Upland Plover, and like that bird frequents the upland fields as well as the shore. No other small Sandpiper is so evenly buff-colored. The Baird's Sandpiper is buffy only across the breast; the throat and belly are white. On the wing, overhead, the wing-linings are seen to be crossed by peculiar black and white scale-marks (see diagram).

MARBLED GODWIT. *Limosa fedoa*.

The Godwits are large shore-birds with long, straight or perceptibly *upturned bills*. The bills of Curlews turn *down*. The uniform *buff-brown* coloration identifies this species.

Hudsonian Godwit. *Limosa hæmastica.*

The large size (larger than the Greater Yellow-legs) and the long, straight or slightly *upturned* bill distinguish this bird as a Godwit; the tail, *ringed broadly with black and white,* proclaims it this species, the 'Ring-tailed Marlin' of the old gunners. In the spring the bird is usually gray-backed and red-breasted; in the fall, gray-backed and whitish-breasted. The Marbled Godwit is, at all times, a mottled buffy-brown.

Flying overhead, the bird shows blackish axillar feathers (where the wings join the body) and smoky wing-linings. No other shore-bird shows a blackish under-wing surface.

Ruff. *Philomachus pugnax.*

No native shore-bird has anything resembling the great loose ruffs about the neck that the male Ruff possesses during the breeding-season. The coloration varies considerably; the ruffs may be black, buff, brown, or white, or a combination of those colors.

Most of the specimens of this European species that have been taken on this side of the Atlantic have been in the more obscure plumages of the female, winter male, and immature. They then resemble, slightly, the similarly sized Upland Plover, but are not streaked on the breast. In flight the whitish outer tail-feathers give the appearance of two *oval* white patches separated by a dark center stripe. American specimens have usually been found in the company of Lesser Yellow-legs. Compared with that bird they are larger (near size of Greater Yellow-legs) and browner. The Yellow-legs would always show a conspicuous white rump.

Sanderling. *Crocethia alba.*

A small, plump Sandpiper with a flashing white stripe in the wing. Other small waders have more or less obscure wing-stripes, but in none of them does the stripe contrast so boldly or extend so far along the wing.

A little larger than a Spotted Sandpiper; usually rusty in the spring; the whitest of the Sandpipers in the fall; bill and legs stout and black; prefers the outer beaches to the mud-flats frequented by most shore-birds.

The note, a short *kip*, is distinctive.

AVOCETS AND STILTS: RECURVIROSTRIDÆ

AVOCET. *Recurvirostra americana.*
In recent years accidental in the East. A very large shore-bird with an *upturned,* somewhat Godwit-like bill. This and the striking coloration, black and white with a pinkish head and neck, set it quite apart from anything else.

BLACK-NECKED STILT. *Himantopus mexicanus.*
A large, slim wader, black above and white below, with *extremely long red legs.* In flight it is white beneath, with black, unpatterned wings. The only pure black and white shore-bird.

PHALAROPES: PHALAROPODIDÆ

Small Sandpiper-like birds with longer necks than most small waders; equally at home wading or swimming.

Two species, the Northern and the Red Phalarope, are most commonly seen out at sea, where, especially in the fall, they much resemble Sanderlings except for their swimming habits. When feeding, they often spin around like tops, rapidly dabbing their thin bills into the roiled water. The females wear the bright colors, the males the dull — an exact reversal of nature's usual order of things.

RED PHALAROPE. *Phalaropus fulicarius.*
The Red Phalarope, while in our latitude, is the most strictly maritime species of the family, rarely occurring inland.

The sea-going habits distinguish it as a Phalarope; in the breeding plumage, the *reddish under parts* (blackish at a distance in poor light) separate it from the Northern.

In the winter plumage, the way we usually see the bird, it is of much the same color as a winter Sanderling, gray and white, but with a characteristic dark '*phalarope-mark*' through the eye. The bird in this plumage is very similar to the Northern Phalarope, but is a little larger and paler. In flight the white wing-stripe of the Red does not contrast so much with the dark gray of the wing. This stripe can, in the Northern, be compared to that of a Sanderling, and, in the Red, to a Piping Plover. As most field students know those two commoner birds well before they have much experience with Phalaropes, the comparison helps. At close range, the *heavier* bill of the Red, yellowish toward the base, and the *yellowish* legs, will identify it positively. The Northern has *black* legs and a more *needle-like* bill.

NORTHERN PHALAROPE. *Lobipes lobatus.*

Should a Sanderling be observed at sea, and should it light upon the water, then it is a Phalarope. The present species is the commonest 'Sea-Snipe' in the East, and the one that is most often likely to appear at inland localities.

In the breeding plumage it is gray above with a patch of *red on the side of the neck*; the Red Phalarope is completely rufous below. In winter plumage, the way we usually see them (even in late summer), the two are much more similar (see Red Phalarope). The Phalarope has a shorter white wing-stripe than the Sanderling and flies with a deeper wing-stroke.

WILSON'S PHALAROPE. *Steganopus tricolor.*

In the breeding plumage the broad neck-stripe of *cinnamon blending into black* is the most conspicuous mark. At a distance in flight it bears a striking resemblance to a Lesser Yellow-legs; it is dark-winged (no wing-stripe as in the other Phalaropes) with a white rump. This similarity is even more striking in the fall plumage, when the bird, as if it were itself mistaken, is sometimes found mixed in with flocks of Yellow-legs. The Phalarope is immaculately white below, with no breast-streaking, and has a thinner, more needle-like bill, and more greenish or straw-colored (not Canary-yellow) legs. The manner when feeding along the margin is very nervous. The swimming and spinning habit, when indulged in, is quite conclusive. Yellow-legs occasionally swim but do not spin and dab.

JAEGERS: STERCORARIIDÆ

The Jaegers are dark hawk-like, or rather, Falcon-like, sea-birds that may occasionally be seen chasing and plundering the numerous Gulls and Terns. Their plumages vary considerably; so we have light phases, birds with dark backs and light under parts; dark phases, birds of uniform dark coloration; and intermediates. One noticeable field character is the *flash of white* displayed in the wing across the base of the primary feathers. This feature and the two *elongated central tail-feathers* will immediately distinguish these birds as Jaegers. Immature birds of the three species are not safely separable in the field.

The Northern Skua belongs to this group, but lacks the long central tail-feathers of the Jaegers. The English call all Jaegers 'Skuas.'

WING OF JAEGER

Showing the flash of white at the base of the primaries

POMARINE JAEGER. *Stercorarius pomarinus.*
This species may be distinguished from the two other Jaegers by the shape of the two long central tail-feathers, which are broad and twisted. It is a larger and heavier-appearing bird than the following species (smaller than a Herring Gull).

PARASITIC JAEGER. *Stercorarius parasiticus.*
This is the commonest Jaeger of the three. The appearance of the pointed central tail-feathers, short compared with those of the other Jaegers, is the best specific character.

LONG-TAILED JAEGER. *Stercorarius longicaudus.*
The extremely long, attenuated central tail-feathers will identify this species.

NORTHERN SKUA. *Catharacta skua.*
A rare sea-bird, seldom observed except on the fishing-banks off our northern coasts.

About the size of a Herring Gull. A large dark brown Hawk-like bird with rusty under parts, a short *square-cut, slightly uptilted tail* and conspicuous *white patches at the base of the primaries*. The smaller, slenderer Jaegers also show white in the primaries. The wings of the Jaegers are long and pointed, while those of the Skua are wider and rounded at the tips.

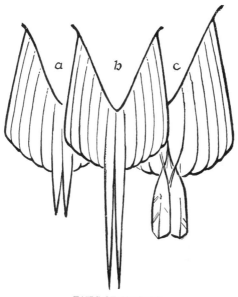

TAILS OF JAEGERS

a. Parasitic   *b*. Long-tailed   *c*. Pomarine

GULLS: LARINÆ

Long-winged swimming birds with superb powers of flight. Gulls differ from Terns in averaging larger, having the bill, which is proportionately shorter, slightly hooked, and the tail square-cut or rounded, rarely forked. Gulls are more robust in form and wider of wing than the Terns. In Gull terminology the word *mantle* is frequently used, meaning the upper surface of the wings and the broad strip of back separating them.

GLAUCOUS GULL. *Larus hyperboreus.*

A large, chalky-white Gull *without dark wing-tips*; larger than the Herring Gull, or about the size of a Black-back.

Immature birds in the first-winter plumage are cream-colored or buffy, but are recognizable as 'white-winged' Gulls by the lack of dark wing-tips. Second-year birds are extremely white.

This species and the next are often confused because of their similarity of coloration. Aside from the difference in size, the best field mark is the bill, which in the Glaucous is much longer and heavier.

ICELAND GULL. *Larus leucopterus.*

Like the Glaucous Gull, *chalky-white without any dark markings*, but differing from that species in size. The Iceland is usually a shade smaller than the Herring Gull, while the Glaucous is much larger. The character of the bill cited above will, with a little practice, easily separate them.

The flight of the Iceland is much lighter and more airy than that of the Glaucous. It might be said of the Gulls as a group that the lightness of their flight is in a ratio to the size of the bird.

GREAT BLACK-BACKED GULL. *Larus marinus.*

Much larger than the Herring Gull. This powerful bird is unmistakable. Even when so far distant that form becomes indistinct, the dark, slaty color of its back and wings stands out as a black spot superimposed on the white of its under parts.

The young birds resemble the corresponding stages of the Herring Gull, but are paler, especially on the head and under parts. The 'saddle-back' pattern, however, is quite evident. The head and bill of the Black-back are noticeably larger, and the flight is more labored.

HERRING GULL. *Larus argentatus smithsonianus.*

This is the common large 'Sea-Gull' of both the interior and the coast. Every beginner in the field study of birds should acquaint himself with this species thoroughly before attempting to recognize the others. It should be the basis of comparison.

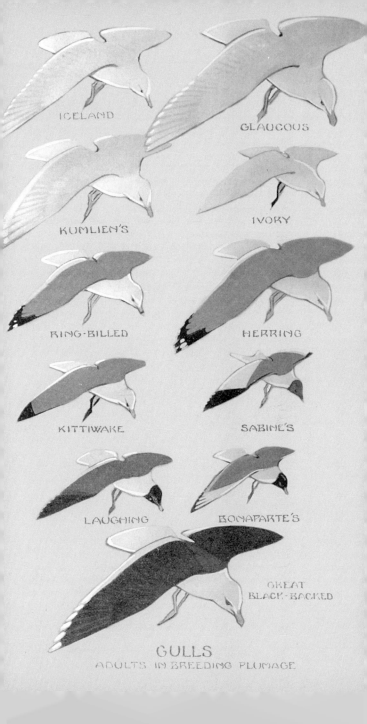

ICELAND

GLAUCOUS

KUMLIEN'S

IVORY

RING-BILLED

HERRING

KITTIWAKE

SABINE'S

LAUGHING

BONAPARTE'S

GREAT
BLACK-BACKED

GULLS
ADULTS IN BREEDING PLUMAGE

The adult is the only large gray-mantled Gull that combines the characteristics of black wing-tips and flesh-colored legs.

The immature bird in the first year is the common dusky brown Gull that one sees in such numbers. No other young Gull is quite so dark and uniform in coloration.

The second-year bird is whiter. The tail is broadly tipped with dark, which blends into the white of the rump.

KUMLIEN'S GULL. *Larus kumlieni.*

Regarded as a hybrid, intermediate between the Herring and Iceland Gulls. The adult is similar in size and appearance to the Herring Gull, but with dark *gray* markings toward tips of wings, instead of black as in that species. The paleness of the bird approaches the chalkiness of the Iceland Gull.

First-year birds resemble first-year Herring Gulls, but are paler, especially on the primaries, or long wing-feathers, which in the Herring are almost blackish.

Second-year birds are pale and buffy, resembling young Iceland Gulls in the first-year plumage, but the primaries, instead of being frosty or whitish, are distinctly grayish — two or three shades darker than the rest of the bird.

RING-BILLED GULL. *Larus delawarensis.*

The adult is almost identical in pattern with the Herring Gull, but it may readily be distinguished by its smaller size, a conspicuous *black ring* on the bill, and *yellowish* or *greenish legs.* In flight the bird is more buoyant than its larger counterpart and shows much more black on the *under side* of the primaries, or long wing-feathers.

The immature bird is often confused with the second-year Herring Gull, which has a semblance of a ring on the bill. One of the best distinguishing features, aside from the size and the color of the legs, is the pattern of the tail. In the Herring Gull the tail terminates in a broad dark band that blends into the whitish color of the rump. The band near the tip of the tail of the Ring-bill is narrower and sharply defined.

LAUGHING GULL. *Larus atricilla.*

Much smaller than the Herring Gull. The Laughing Gull

may be distinguished in any plumage from the other small Gulls by its *dark mantle* and the conspicuous *white border* that lines the hind edge of the wings. This is the common black-hooded Gull that is found in summer on our Atlantic and Gulf coasts. In winter the head is white with dark markings. Fall transitional plumages are often confusing.

The immature bird is dusky-gray with a *white rump*. It is the only small Gull with a dark breast.

FRANKLIN'S GULL. *Larus pipixcan.*

The Franklin's Gull, a bird of the prairies, is purely accidental in the Eastern States, and its close resemblance to both the Bonaparte's and the Laughing Gulls makes sight identifi-

WING OF FRANKLIN'S GULL

cation a highly risky procedure. In summer plumage the head is black, but in winter, which is the season when strays would be most apt to appear in the East, the head is white, with a dark patch extending from the eye around the back of the nape. The Franklin's Gull has some very sharply defined black markings which form an uneven band toward the tips of the wings, whereas the black in the outer primaries of the Laughing Gull blends quite evenly into the dark gray of the rest of the wing. The diagram explains it. The wrists and outer primaries of the Bonaparte's are largely white; in the Franklin's they are mostly gray.

BONAPARTE'S GULL. *Larus philadelphia.*

About half the size of a Herring Gull. The little Bonaparte's Gull may be identified at a great distance in any plumage by the characteristic wing-pattern created by the *white outer primaries*, which contrast strikingly with the gray of the mantle.

In the breeding plumage this species has a black head. In winter adults and immature birds the head is white with a conspicuous black spot behind the eye. Immature birds have a narrow black band on the tip of the tail.

LITTLE GULL. *Larus minutus.*

A European species that has been detected a few times on our side of the Atlantic.

The Little Gull shows some resemblance to the Bonaparte's Gull and seems to prefer the company of that species while with us. It averages about two inches smaller than the Bonaparte's, from which it may be distinguished by the gray, unpatterned wings devoid of black tips. The best field character is the *blackish, or sooty, under surface* of the wings.

IVORY GULL. *Pagophila alba.*

This Arctic species, which is of very rare occurrence in the United States, is the only pure-white Gull with *black* legs. It differs from the other two 'white-winged' Gulls (Gulls without dark wing-tips), the Iceland and the Glaucous, in being smaller than either (nearer the size of a large Pigeon), with black, instead of flesh-colored, legs. The wings are comparatively slender, and the flight is quite Tern-like.

Immature birds are similar to the adults, but are marked with a few dusky spots about the head, wings, and tail.

KITTIWAKE. *Rissa tridactyla tridactyla.*

The Kittiwake is best known as an 'off-shore' Gull of the ocean, smaller than either the Herring or Ring-billed, which it resembles in coloration. The legs of the Kittiwake are *black*, whereas those of the Herring and Ring-billed Gulls are flesh-colored and yellowish respectively. Another good point is the appearance of the black wing-tips, which are cut *straight across*, as if they had been dipped in ink.

The immature bird has a dark bar on the back of the neck and a black band on the end of the tail. It is most likely to be confused with the Bonaparte's Gull in the same plumage, but

the Kittiwake has a dark bar on the back of the neck, instead
of a dark spot behind the eye, and has more black in the outer
primaries and the *fore border* of the wing.

SABINE'S GULL. *Xema sabini.*
About the size of the Bonaparte's Gull. The only American
Gull with a *forked* tail. The jet-black outer primaries and the
conspicuous triangular white patch on the hind edge of the
wing create a distinctive wing-pattern that renders this rare
little Gull unmistakable. The head is dark only in the
breeding plumage.

TERNS: STERNINÆ

The Terns are Gull-like sea-birds, differing from the Gulls in
being more slender in build, narrower of wing, and more graceful in flight. The bill is considerably slenderer and sharper-
pointed, usually held pointed downward toward the water.
The tail is usually forked. Most Terns are white, or whitish,
with black caps. In winter this cap is more or less imperfect,
the black of the forehead being largely replaced by white.
A typical Tern habit is to plunge head first into the water
Kingfisher-fashion.

GULL-BILLED TERN. *Gelochelidon nilotica aranea.*
Somewhat larger and paler and with tail less forked than
the Common Tern; feet black. The *stout*, almost Gull-like,
black bill is, perhaps, the best field mark.
The call, a high *kik-kik-kik* is responsible for the nickname
'Laughing Swallow.'

FORSTER'S TERN. *Sterna forsteri.*
Very similar to the Common Tern in size and appearance.
White, with a pale gray mantle and black cap; bill and feet
orange-red; tail deeply forked.
Winter plumage: — Similar, but without the black cap; instead, a heavy black spot, like an ear-cap, on the side of the
whitish head.
This species in adult plumage is generally considered very
difficult to identify in the field because of its close resemblance

LAUGHING
IMM.

RING-BILLED
IMM.

HERRING
FIRST YEAR

HERRING
SECOND YEAR

KUMLIEN'S
FIRST YEAR

GREAT BLACK-BACKED
IMM.

KITTIWAKE
IMM.

SABINE'S
IMM.

BELOW

ABOVE

LITTLE
ADULTS IN WINTER PLUMAGE

BONAPARTE'S
IMM.

GULLS

to the Common Tern, but with a little practice it actually becomes an easy matter. The tail of the Forster's is of nearly the same tone of gray as the back and wings; that of the Common is a clear white that contrasts strikingly with the gray of the back. This difference is quite evident when the birds wheel and flash in the sunlight. Then, too, the primaries of the Forster's are *silvery*, in direct contrast to those of the Common, which are dusky.

Immature birds may be easily separated by another character. The Forster's Tern has a black patch through the eye and ear, while in the Common Tern this same dark area extends from the eye clear around the back of the head.

The call-note of the present species is a harsh, nasal *za-a-ap* that has been likened to the ripping of cloth.

COMMON TERN. *Sterna hirundo hirundo.*
Less than half the size of a Herring Gull. This is the small black-capped Gull-like bird that the fishermen call 'Mackerel Gull' or 'Medrick.' As its name indicates, it is the commonest species of Tern that we have.
Adult in breeding plumage: — White, with a light-gray mantle and black cap; bill orange-red with a black tip; feet orange-red; tail deeply forked.
Immature and winter adult: — Similar, without the black cap; instead, a black band extending from the eye around the back of the head.
The call-note is a drawling *kee-arr.*

ARCTIC TERN. *Sterna paradisæa.*
The Arctic Tern is famous for having the most lengthy migration of any bird. From its summer home in the northern parts of the Northern Hemisphere it migrates to the Antarctic, where it spends our northern winter, but, strangely, it is seldom noted in migration on the Atlantic coast south of their southernmost breeding-grounds in New England.
Adult: — Very difficult to distinguish from the Common Tern. Grayish-white with a darker gray mantle, black cap, and *blood-red* feet and bill; tail deeply forked. A good mark is the *white streak below the black cap.* In the Common the whole face is clear white.

The Arctic Tern is *grayer* than any of the other species which it closely resembles. The bill is blood-red *to the tip*, whereas that of the Roseate is largely black, and those of the Common and Forster's are orange-red, *usually* tipped with black. The tarsi of the Arctic Tern are shorter than those of the others, so when the bird is at rest with Common Terns, it sits lower. The tail is longer and more streaming than that of the Common (projecting slightly beyond the wing-tips when at rest), and the flight is more willowy. The call-note is similar, but ends in a *rising inflection*.

Immature birds are quite indistinguishable except possibly by the length of the tarsus.

ROSEATE TERN. *Sterna dougalli dougalli.*
Adult: — About the size of the Common Tern. White, with a very pale gray mantle, black cap, *black bill*, and red feet; tail very deeply forked.

The black or largely black bill sets it apart from the other similar species: the Common, Forster's, and Arctic Terns all have reddish bills. The Roseate, when detected, is usually found with the more abundant Common Tern. At a distance, in flight, it appears whiter than that species and the wing-stroke is much deeper. Close inspection will reveal the black bill and the extremely long, outer tail-feathers. At rest, the tail-tips of the Roseate Tern extend far beyond the wing-tips, while in the Common, this is just the reverse.

The call-note of the Roseate Tern is a rasping *ka-a-ak*, louder and harsher than the drawling *kee-arr* of the Common Tern. It also has a musical two-syllabled call, *chirry* or *chivy*, vaguely suggestive of the Semipalmated Plover. This note, which is constantly uttered, is far more useful in identifying immature birds in the fall than any possible mark.

SOOTY TERN. *Sterna fuscata fuscata.*
The Sooty Tern is essentially a bird of tropical shores, but occasionally individuals are driven northward by West Indian hurricanes. After tropical storms of unusual severity a few individuals even reach the New England coast.
Adult: — Upper parts sooty black; under parts white; cheeks and patch on the forehead white; bill and feet black.

The only Tern that is black above and white below (the dissimilar Black Skimmer gives the same effect at a distance).

Immature: — Brown all over; lighter on the under parts; back spotted with white.

BRIDLED TERN. *Sterna anæthetus.*

Although this bird has rarely been taken in the United States, it should be looked for after tropical storms. Undoubtedly it has occurred more often on the southern Atlantic coast than the records would indicate. It resembles slightly the Sooty Tern — dusky above and white below — but has a wide *whitish collar* separating the black of the cap from the dark of the back.

LEAST TERN. *Sterna antillarum antillarum.*

The smallest of the Terns — about eight and one half inches long.

Adult: — White, with a pale-gray mantle and black cap; white patch on forehead; bill and feet *yellow.* The extremely small size and the yellowish bill and feet render identification certain.

The immature bird may be mistaken for the fall Black Tern, but is smaller, with a *whitish*, instead of dark, tail. Young Common Terns, with their rather short tails and white foreheads, might possibly be mistaken for Least Terns, but they always show a great deal more black about the shoulder of the wing.

ROYAL TERN. *Thalasseus maximus maximus.*

Slightly smaller than the Herring Gull and the Caspian Tern; white, with a pale-gray mantle, black cap, large red bill, and deeply forked tail.

The more deeply forked tail and the more slender bill are the best field marks by which to differentiate the bird from the similar Caspian Tern, which has a moderately forked tail. At rest the wing-tips of the Caspian extend well beyond the end of the tail; those of the Royal barely reach the tail-tip.

CABOT'S TERN. *Thalasseus sandvicensis acuflavida.*

Slightly larger and more slender than the Common Tern.

White, with a pale-gray mantle and black cap; black feathers on back of crown somewhat elongated, giving the bird a crested appearance at times; bill long and slender, *black with a yellow tip;* feet black.

The yellow-tipped black bill is as good a field mark as any; it is easy to see and marks the bird immediately.

CASPIAN TERN. *Hydroprogne caspia imperator.*

About the size of a Herring Gull, from which it may be distinguished by its black cap, red bill, and forked tail. The great size and large red bill will set this species apart from all the others of this group except the Royal Tern. The tail of the Caspian is forked for only a quarter of its length; that of the Royal for fully half its length. The Caspian Tern has a fairly general distribution over most of the Eastern States as a migrant on the larger bodies of water, but the Royal is confined more to the coasts of the Southern States. In the large Tern colonies of the South, where both birds may be found together, this species may be distinguished readily at long range from the more numerous Royal Terns by the greater amount of dark in the primaries. The call-note of this species is a deep, raucous *ka-arr*, much deeper than the corresponding note of the Royal.

BLACK TERN. *Chlidonias nigra surinamensis.*

Breeding plumage: — Head and under parts black; back and wings gray; under tail-coverts white. In this plumage it is the only *black-bodied Tern.*

Immature and adult in winter: — Head and under parts white; back and wings gray; dark markings on head, about eye, ear, and back of neck. The winter plumage comes very early; mottled, changing birds appear in midsummer. In this pied plumage the short tail and deeply swooping wing-beats are good points.

NODDY. *Anous stolidus stolidus.*

A West Indian species, breeding in this country only on the Florida Keys. Like the Sooty Tern, it is sometimes driven north by tropical hurricanes.

Uniformly brown, with a whitish head; the only *brown* Tern

TERNS and SKIMMERS

(except the immature Sooty) and the only Tern with a *rounded* tail. The whitish cap on a dark bird gives a reverse or 'negative' effect of the other Terns with their dark caps and light bodies.

SKIMMERS: RHYNCHOPIDÆ

The remarkably specialized bill sets the Skimmers apart. The lower mandible is considerably longer than the upper. Otherwise Skimmers bear a slight superficial resemblance to the Terns, but they do not have the graceful powers of flight of those birds. Their wings are extremely long proportionally. In North America this group is represented by one species.

BLACK SKIMMER. *Rhynchops nigra nigra.*
Smaller and more slender than the Herring Gull; upper parts black; under parts white; bill long and flat (vertically), red, tipped with black; *lower mandible nearly a third longer than the upper.*
The black and white coloration in connection with the unusual scissor-like bill identifies the Skimmer. It is a purely maritime species, usually seen skimming over the water, dipping its long lower mandible for small fish and other food particles; hence its name.

AUKS, MURRES, AND PUFFINS: ALCIDÆ

Birds of this group frequent the open sea and only rarely appear on fresh water. They are all quite northern in distribution and descend to the latitude of the Northern States mainly in winter. The best time to watch for them from vantage-points along the coast is during nasty weather, when a few individuals are sometimes blown close inshore.
They are Ducklike in appearance, but may be distinguished by their short necks, and pointed, or deep and compressed, bills. When flying, they beat their wings very rapidly on account of the narrow wing-arc, and are given to much circling and veering, seldom holding the straight course of a Duck.

RAZOR-BILLED AUK. *Alca torda.*
Similar to the Brünnich's Murre in all its plumages, black

above and white below; differentiated by its heavier head, and its deep and compressed bill which is crossed midway by a conspicuous *white* mark. On the water the *cocked wren-like tail* of the Razor-bill is characteristic.

ATLANTIC, *or* COMMON, MURRE. *Uria aalge aalge.*

The Atlantic, or Common, Murre, notwithstanding its name, is a very rare bird within the limits of the United States. It is safely separable in the field from the Brünnich's Murre only if observed at close quarters. It will then be seen that the bill is longer and more slender. The Brünnich's Murre has a *flesh-colored stripe* along the base of the bill near the gape, a mark that the Common Murre lacks. In winter plumage the Atlantic Murre has a narrow black line running back from the eye into the white of the cheek — a very good field mark.

RINGED MURRE.

This phase of the Atlantic Murre is distinguished by a narrow white ring about the eye and a short white line extending back from the eye on the side of the head.

BRÜNNICH'S MURRE. *Uria lomvia lomvia.*

This is the only Alcid one is likely to encounter in the interior. Size of a small Duck.

Breeding plumage: — Head, neck, back, and wings *dark*; under parts and line on the hind edge of the wing *white*; bill *pointed*.

Winter plumage: — Similar, but white on the throat and side of face.

The only common species with which the Brünnich's Murre may be easily confused is the Razor-billed Auk. The bill of the Murre is slender, whereas the bill of the Razor-bill is deep and flattened. On the water the longer tail of the Razor-bill is often cocked up in the air.

DOVEKIE. *Alle alle.*

About the size of a Starling. This is by far the smallest of our wintering sea-birds. Its contrasting Alcid pattern, *black above and white below*, together with its *small size*, renders it quite unlike anything else.

BLACK GUILLEMOT. *Cepphus grylle grylle.*

About the size of a Horned Grebe, or of our smallest Ducks.

BLACK GUILLEMOT

SUMMER   WINTER

PUFFIN
WINTER

DOVEKIE
WINTER

RAZOR-BILLED AUK

SUMMER   WINTER

BRÜNNICH'S MURRE

SUMMER   WINTER

BRÜNNICH'S   COMMON   "RINGED"

MURRES

ALCIDAE

Most beginners imagine that should they come upon this species along the coast during the winter months, they will be confronted by a bird very similar to a White-winged Scoter in appearance, black with white wing-patches. Sometimes the enthusiast will even metamorphose a White-winged Scoter into a Guillemot. It is during the breeding-season that they have this striking black and white plumage, although it is said that occasional birds retain it through the winter. The Guillemot may be distinguished from the Scoter by its very much smaller size and slender, *pointed* bill. The wing-patches of the Guillemot are placed farther forward, are larger, and show much more plainly as the bird rides the water.

When in winter plumage the bird is quite unlike anything else, but it has been pointed out that at a distance on the water it bears some resemblance to an Old-squaw Duck (because of its pied pattern). As it is largely white at this season, it does not justify its name of Black Guillemot. In this plumage the under parts are white, the back is dusky and whitish, and the wings are black with large white patches, as in summer. Immature birds are darker above than adults.

MANDT'S GUILLEMOT. *Cepphus grylle mandti.*

This subspecies is more northerly in distribution than the last and seldom reaches the latitude of the States.

Like the Black Guillemot, but the greater wing-coverts are white *to their bases.* As this difference would not be very evident in the field, sight records of such birds would not be very convincing.

ATLANTIC PUFFIN. *Fratercula arctica arctica.*

The most striking feature of this chunky little sea-bird is its amazing *triangular* bill.

Breeding plumage: — Upper parts black; under parts and cheeks white; triangular bill broadly tipped with red.

Winter plumage: — Similar, but cheeks grayer.

PIGEONS AND DOVES: COLUMBIDÆ

Two types of Pigeons occur in North America; those with fanlike tails, of which the Domestic Pigeon is the most familiar, and the slimmer, brownish type with short rounded or long pointed tails. The Mourning Dove is the most characteristic of the latter group.

WHITE-CROWNED PIGEON. *Columba leucocephala.*
Occurs in Florida; about the build of a Domestic Pigeon; uniformly dark with a *white or whitish* crown. (Could possibly be confused with the Noddy.)

ROCK DOVE, *or* DOMESTIC PIGEON. *Columba livia.*
This bird has become feral in places and is as firmly established as a wild species as the House Sparrow or the Starling. It needs no description.

ZENAIDA DOVE. *Zenaida zenaida zenaida.*
A rare West-Indian species, probably occasional on the Florida Keys; like a Mourning Dove, but tail *square*, broadly tipped with pearl gray; wing with a *white stripe* on the hind edge.

MOURNING DOVE

EASTERN MOURNING DOVE. *Zenaidura macroura carolinensis.*
A small *brown* Pigeon, smaller and slimmer than a Domestic

Dove, with a *pointed,* not fan-shaped, tail; the common Wild Dove of the East.

The call from which the bird derives its name is a mournful *ooah-cooo — cooo — coo.* At a distance only the last three coos are audible.

The Passenger Pigeon is now pretty definitely known to be extinct, but still the reports of individuals *seen* are frequently brought to our attention. In every case the Mourning Dove is undoubtedly the bird in question. The Passenger Pigeon was much larger, with a longer tail and longer wings and a *blue-gray* head. The head of the Mourning Dove is buffy brown with a *black spot* behind the eye. The rapidly beating wings of the Dove produce a whistling sound; the flight of the Wild Pigeon was silent.

WHITE-WINGED DOVE. *Melopelia asiatica.*
The White-winged Dove, a species of accidental occurrence in the East, might best be described as a Mourning Dove with a *rounded* tail and a large *white patch* on the wing.

EASTERN GROUND DOVE. *Columbigallina passerina passerina.*
A very small Dove, *not much larger than a Sparrow,* with wings that flash *rufous-red* in flight.
THE BAHAMAN GROUND DOVE. *Columbigallina passerina bahamensis.*
The variety found in Bermuda.

KEY WEST QUAIL-DOVE. *Oreopeleia chrysea.*
Slightly larger than the Mourning Dove, with a rounded tail, *rufous* upper parts, and a *whitish* belly.

CUCKOOS, ANIS, ETC.: CUCULIDÆ

The Cuckoos are slim, long-tailed, sinuous-looking birds, a little longer than the Robin, dull olive-brown above and whitish below. Anis are loose-jointed and Cuckoo-like in appearance, but are coal-black with deep, high-ridged bills.

MAYNARD'S CUCKOO. *Coccyzus minor maynardi.*
A resident of the mangrove swamps of southern Florida; like

the Yellow-billed Cuckoo, but the under parts are a strong *yellowish buff*.

YELLOW-BILLED CUCKOO. *Coccyzus americanus americanus.*
Known as a Cuckoo by the slim proportions and brown and white coloration; distinguished from the Black-bill by the presence of *rufous* in the wings, the *large* white spots at the tips of the tail-feathers, and, at close range, the *yellow* lower mandible of the bill.

BLACK-BILLED CUCKOO. *Coccyzus erythrophthalmus.* (See Yellow-billed Cuckoo.)

SMOOTH-BILLED ANI. *Crotophaga ani.*
The Anis are coal-black Cuckoo-like birds, about the size of the Florida Purple Grackle, with loose-jointed tails, short wings (hence a weak flight), and a deep bill with a *high, curved ridge* on the upper mandible. The peculiar bill-formation gives the bird a decidedly Parrot-like or Puffin-like profile. Of the two species that are found occasionally in the southernmost portions of the United States, the Smooth-billed variety is most frequently observed.

GROOVE-BILLED ANI. *Crotophaga sulcirostris sulcirostris.*
Like the Smooth-billed Ani, but with *three grooves* on the upper mandible.
The notes of the two species are different: the Smooth-billed bird has a long-drawn, complaining whistle, quite unlike the rapidly uttered notes of the present species.

OWLS: TYTONIDÆ AND STRIGIDÆ

Nocturnal birds of prey, characterized by the large head, large eyes, *facial disks*, and soft, moth-like, noiseless flight. They seem quite neckless. Some species have conspicuous feather tufts, or 'horns'; others are round-headed, devoid of such ornamentation.

BARN OWL. *Tyto alba pratincola.*
A long-legged, light-colored Owl with a *white heart-shaped face*.

MOCKINGBIRD

BROWN
THRASHER

KINGFISHER
MALE

NORTHERN
SHRIKE

CATBIRD

YELLOW-
BILLED
CUCKOO

BLACK-
BILLED
CUCKOO

BLUE-GRAY
GNATCATCHER

GOLDEN-CROWNED
KINGLET

BLACK-CAPPED
CHICKADEE

BROWN
CREEPER

RUBY-CROWNED
KINGLET

TUFTED
TITMOUSE

BROWN-HEADED
NUTHATCH

RED-BREASTED
NUTHATCH

WHITE-BREASTED
NUTHATCH

It may be distinguished in flight at a distance; as an Owl, by the large head and light, moth-like flight; as this species, by the whitish under parts and buffy upper plumage (Short-ear would be buffy-brown above and below).

EASTERN SCREECH OWL. *Otus asio nævius.*
The only *small* Owl with ear-tufts. Two color phases occur: red-brown and gray.
The call is a mournful, quavering whinny, or wail, quite unlike the vocal effort of any other species.

THE FLORIDA SCREECH OWL (*Otus asio floridanus*) is the resident subspecies of peninsular Florida, while the SOUTHERN SCREECH OWL (*Otus asio asio*) is the bird that from Georgia and Louisiana to Virginia and southern Illinois fills the gap between the Florida and the northern forms.

GREAT HORNED OWL. *Bubo virginianus virginianus.*
The only *large* Owl (nearly two feet in length) with ear-tufts, or 'horns.' The Long-eared Owl is much smaller (fifteen inches; Crow-sized in flight), with lengthwise streakings, rather than crosswise barrings, beneath. In flight this Owl is larger than even our largest Buteo Hawks (Red-tail, etc.); is darker, looks neckless, and is larger-headed. The Barred Owl at a distance appears grayer, not so brown.
The hooting of the Great Horned Owl is deeper and more resonant than that of the Barred Owl and consists of three, four, or six hoots, not eight.

ARCTIC HORNED OWL. *Bubo virginianus subarcticus.*
Like the Great Horned Owl, but grayer; occasional individuals are almost as white as Snowy Owls. The facial disks are *pale gray*, not chestnut-brown as in the common form.

LABRADOR HORNED OWL. *Bubo virginianus heterocnemis.*
Like the Great Horned Owl, but darker and more heavily barred beneath. The barring often obliterates completely the white markings, giving the bird a black-breasted appearance.

SNOWY OWL. *Nyctea nyctea.*
A large *white* Owl with a round head. The White Gyrfalcon is smaller-headed, has *pointed* wings, and flies with quicker, more vigorous strokes. The Arctic Horned Owl has ear-tufts, and is a woodland, not an open-country, bird.

Young Owls of all species are white or whitish before the feathers replace the down. Even though their extreme youth is quite apparent, they are often dubbed 'Snowy' Owls. Even in callow youngsters of this sort, the resemblance to their progenitors is already visible; stubby ear-tufts adorn the fuzzy heads of baby Great Horned Owls, while the heart-shaped faces of Barn Owls reflect their parentage.

AMERICAN HAWK OWL. *Surnia ulula caparoch.*
A medium-sized, diurnal Owl, with a long, Falcon-like tail; smaller than a Crow; maintains a more inclined body-posture at rest, not so upright as other Owls; often perches at the tip-top of a pine tree or in some other exposed situation and bobs its tail in the manner of a Sparrow Hawk.

FLORIDA BURROWING OWL. *Speotyto cunicularia floridana.*
A small brown *ground* Owl; about the size of a Screech Owl, earless and with *very long legs* (for an Owl); resident of the prairie regions of the Florida peninsula. The only *small* 'earless' Owl in Florida.

NORTHERN BARRED OWL. *Strix varia varia.*
The Barred Owl is the common large gray-brown earless Owl of the woodlands, the Owl with the puffy round head. The large liquid brown eyes (all others except the Barn Owl have yellow eyes), and the manner of the streaking and barring — barred *crosswise* on the breast and streaked *lengthwise* on the belly — will identify the bird at closer range.

The call is less deep than that of the Great Horned Owl. It usually consists of eight hoots (hence the nickname 'Eight-hooter'), in two groups of four: *hoo-hoo-hoo-hoo ... hoo-hoo-hoo-hooah.* The *ah* at the close is especially characteristic. Distorted by distance, the hooting sounds like the barking of a dog.

FLORIDA BARRED OWL (*Strix varia alleni*).
Occurs from southern North Carolina and northern Alabama and Mississippi south.

GREAT GRAY OWL. *Scotiaptex nebulosa nebulosa.*
The largest of the Owls, larger than the Great Horned;

SCREECH

GREAT HORNED

LONG-EARED

BARN

SNOWY

BARRED

SHORT-EARED

GREAT GRAY

SAW-WHET

RICHARDSON'S

HAWK

OWLS

resembles the much smaller Barred Owl in coloration; like that bird, it is round-headed, without ear-tufts, but the eyes are *yellow*, not brown, and there is no conspicuous cross-barring on the upper breast. The facial discs are much larger proportionately than those of the Barred Owl. They come to the top of the head as the bird sits and are outlined against the sky.

LONG-EARED OWL. *Asio wilsonianus.*

A Crow-sized Owl with long ear-tufts and a rusty-red face; much smaller than the Great Horned Owl, streaked *lengthwise*, rather than barred crosswise, beneath. The 'ears' are situated close together toward the center of the forehead, giving the bird an entirely different aspect. In flight the ear-tufts are pressed flat against the head; then the bird resembles the similarly proportioned Short-eared Owl, but the large amount of gray in the plumage will separate it at once from the much buffier Short-ear.

SHORT-EARED OWL. *Asio flammeus flammeus.*

A diurnal Owl of the marshes; nearly the size of a Crow. The buffy-brown color and the easy, flitting flight, like that of a large moth, identify it. It might possibly be mistaken for a Rough-legged Hawk; both birds have the same reedlike streaked pattern, both frequent open country, and in flight they both show the large black 'thumb-print' at the base of the primaries on the under surface of the wings; an interesting example of parallel development in two dissimilar types occupying a similar habitat. The Owl is much smaller, with a somewhat slovenly flight, and appears quite big-headed and neckless.

RICHARDSON'S OWL. *Cryptoglaux funerea richardsoni.*

Near the size of a Screech Owl, but *earless*. The even smaller Saw-whet is the only species that much resembles it. The facial discs of the Richardson's Owl are *framed with black*, and the bill is *yellowish* (Saw-whet, black). A point of lesser importance is the white spotting on the forehead.

COMMON SAW-WHET OWL. *Cryptoglaux acadica acadica.*

A very small, ridiculously tame little Owl; much smaller

than the Screech Owl and *without* ear-tufts. The only Owl that resembles it, the Richardson's, is extremely rare within the limits of the Northeastern States.

GOATSUCKERS: CAPRIMULGIDÆ

The Goatsuckers are ample-tailed nocturnal birds with small bills and weak, tiny feet. During the day they rest horizontally on some limb, or on the ground, where their mottled brown pattern blends with the surroundings.

CHUCK-WILL'S-WIDOW. *Antrostomus carolinensis.*
Like the Whip-poor-will, but larger, without as clear a white ring below the throat.

The call is a *chuck'-will-will*, less vigorous than the corresponding efforts of the Whip-poor-will. The accent is on the *first* syllable: in the Whip-poor-will's call it is on the last.

EASTERN WHIP-POOR-WILL. *Antrostomus vociferus vociferus.*
On warm summer evenings we may hear the vigorous cry of the Whip-poor-will, oft-repeated in endless succession. We never hear the notes or see the bird abroad in its search for insects by daylight, as we frequently notice the Nighthawk. When we are fortunate enough to discover it during the day, it springs from its hiding-place and flits away like a large brown moth. If it be a male, the white tail-feathers flash out; if a female, it appears all brown; never does it show the white wing-patches so characteristic of the Nighthawk.

EASTERN NIGHTHAWK. *Chordeiles minor minor.*
The Nighthawk is the slender, slim-winged bird that we see flying erratically about in its hunt for insects high in the air. A nasal *peent,* uttered every now and then, seems to be about all the bird is capable of by way of vocal performance. Occasionally, having attained a height, it folds its wings and dives earthward, zooming up sharply at the end of the drop. The *broad white patch* across the wing is the Nighthawk's mark.

FLORIDA NIGHTHAWK. *Chordeiles minor chapmani.*
The form that breeds in the low-lying coastal country of the

South Atlantic and Gulf States from North Carolina south, and north along the Mississippi valley to southern Illinois.

SWIFTS: MICROPODIDÆ

CHIMNEY SWIFT. *Chætura pelagica.*
A blackish Swallow-like bird with no apparent tail (occasionally it does spread its tail). The best simile, and one

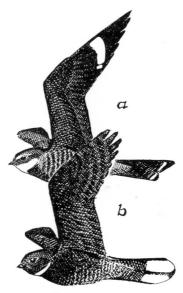

a. NIGHTHAWK, *male*   *b.* WHIP-POOR-WILL, *male*

that is often applied to it, is a 'cigar with wings.' Unlike the Swallows, and most other birds for that matter, it does not appear to beat its wings in unison, but *alternately* — such is the illusion at least. The effect is quite batlike. It frequently sails between spurts, holding its wings *bowed* in a very characteristic manner.

HUMMINGBIRDS: TROCHILIDÆ

RUBY-THROATED HUMMINGBIRD. *Archilochus colubris.*
Hummingbirds need no description. The present species is the only one that occurs in the East. Large Hawk Moths (Sphingidæ) might be mistaken for Hummers, but their visits to the flowers seldom take place much before dusk.

KINGFISHERS: ALCEDINIDÆ

EASTERN BELTED KINGFISHER. *Megaceryle alcyon alcyon.*
It hardly seems necessary to describe the Kingfisher; hovering above the water in readiness for the plunge, or flying with peculiar uneven wing-beats, rattling as it goes, it is one of the first birds that every novice learns. Perched, it is a big-headed bird, larger than a Robin, with a ragged crest and one (male) or two (female) broad breast-bands.

WOODPECKERS: PICIDÆ

Tree-climbing birds, with stiff, spiny tails which act as props in their upward progress. The flight of most species is undulating, produced by several quick beats and a pause. Most species have some amount of red on the head.

NORTHERN FLICKER. *Colaptes auratus luteus.*
Our only *brown* Woodpecker; flight deeply undulating; overhead, shows considerable *yellow* under the wings and tail. The conspicuous *white rump*, visible as the bird flies up, is the best field mark at a distance.

SOUTHERN FLICKER. *Colaptes auratus auratus.*
Found from North Carolina and southern Illinois south.

NORTHERN PILEATED WOODPECKER. *Ceophlœus pileatus abieticola.*
A very large, *Crow-sized* Woodpecker with a conspicuous red *crest*. The great size, bounding flight, and flashing black and white coloration identify it at a distance. The diggings, large *rectangular*, not round, holes, are certain evidence of its presence. The common call resembles that of a Flicker, but is

WHITE BACKS

LARGE BILL

SMALL BILL

HAIRY

DOWNY

BROWN BACK

WHITE RUMP

FLICKER

SCARLET CREST

LONG WHITE
WING PATCH

SAPSUCKER

RED CAP
ZEBRA BACK

RED · BELLIED

RED HEAD

BROAD WHITE
WING PATCH

PILEATED

BLACK CAP
ZEBRA BACK

RED · HEADED

RED · COCKADED

YELLOW CROWNS
(MALES)

BLACK
BACK

LADDER
BACK

ARCTIC
THREE-TOED

AMERICAN
THREE · TOED

BARRED FLANKS

WOODPECKERS

louder, more ringing, and often more hesitant — *kuk* — *kuk-kuk-kuk* —— *kuk* — *kuk*, etc.

SOUTHERN PILEATED WOODPECKER. *Ceophlœus pileatus pileatus.*

Occurs from southeastern Pennsylvania and Illinois south.

FLORIDA PILEATED WOODPECKER. *Ceophlœus pileatus floridanus.*

Found in peninsular Florida, south of Orange County.

RED-BELLIED WOODPECKER. *Centurus carolinus.*

The only *zebra-backed* Woodpecker with a *red* cap. The whole crown of the head is red in the male; the female is red on the nape only.

RED-HEADED WOODPECKER. *Melanerpes erythrocephalus.*

The only Woodpecker with the *entire* head red. Most other species have a *patch* of red somewhere or other on the head. At a distance in flight it appears as a black and white Woodpecker with large square white wing-patches.

The immature bird is brown-headed; the large white wing-patches identify it.

YELLOW-BELLIED SAPSUCKER. *Sphyrapicus varius varius.*

Best identified in all plumages by the *longitudinal white patch* on the black wing. It is our only Woodpecker with a red *forehead* patch. *Males* have red throats; *females*, white.

EASTERN HAIRY WOODPECKER. *Dryobates villosus villosus.*

The Downy and the Hairy are our only *white-backed* Woodpeckers. They are almost identical in pattern, checkered and spotted with black and white; the *males* with a small red patch on the back of the head; the *females*, without.

The Hairy is like a magnified Downy; it is much larger; the bill is especially large, all out of size-relation to the Downy's little 'bark-sticker.' The Downy's song is a series of notes descending in pitch; the Hairy speaks on the same pitch. Lastly, the Downy says *pik;* the Hairy, *peek!*

SOUTHERN HAIRY WOODPECKER. *Dryobates villosus auduboni.*

Like the preceding, but dingier-colored on the breast;

occurs from southeastern Virginia and southern Illinois south.

NORTHERN HAIRY WOODPECKER. *Dryobates villosus septentrionalis.*

A larger form of the Hairy, with more white in the plumage; breeds from central Ontario north.

NEWFOUNDLAND WOODPECKER. *Dryobates villosus terrænovæ.*

The Hairy of Newfoundland; larger and blacker.

NORTHERN DOWNY WOODPECKER. *Dryobates pubescens medianus.* (See Hairy Woodpecker.)

SOUTHERN DOWNY WOODPECKER. *Dryobates pubescens pubescens.*

Like the preceding, but browner on the under parts. This dinginess, when first noted by early ornithologists, was attributed to the smoke from burning pine forests. Present from North Carolina south.

RED-COCKADED WOODPECKER. *Dryobates borealis.*

A *zebra-backed* Woodpecker with a *black* cap; resident of the southern pine forests. Our only other zebra-backed Woodpecker, the Red-belly, has a *red* cap.

ARCTIC THREE-TOED WOODPECKER. *Picoides arcticus.*

A Woodpecker with a white breast and a *solid black* back. The male has a *yellow* crown-patch which the female lacks.

The two Three-toed Woodpeckers inhabit the deep coniferous forests of the North; there their presence can be detected by large patches scaled from the trunks of dead conifers.

AMERICAN THREE-TOED WOODPECKER. *Picoides tridactylus bacatus.*

The males of the two Three-toed Woodpeckers are the only species of the family with *yellow* caps. The '*ladder-back*' will separate this species from the black-backed Arctic Three-toed. The female lacks the yellow cap and resembles the Hairy Woodpecker, but the *barred* flanks and back identify it (Hairy has white down the center of the back). Rarely, aberrant immature specimens of the Hairy Woodpecker have yellowish or orange caps and so are sometimes transmogrified into Three-toed Woodpeckers.

IVORY-BILLED WOODPECKER. *Campephilus principalis.*

Extremely rare; resident of the cypress swamps of the Gulf Coast; a very large Woodpecker, larger than a Crow; *male* with a flaming red crest; *female* with a black crest; might be known from the Florida Pileated Woodpecker by its superior size, *ivory-white bill,* and large white wing-patches *visible when the bird is at rest.* (Pileated has much white in the wing in flight, but this does not show when the bird is climbing.)

The call of the Ivory-bill suggests somewhat the *yank — yank — yank* of the White-breasted Nuthatch.

FLYCATCHERS: TYRANNIDÆ

Birds of this family usually perch in an upright attitude on exposed twigs or branches, from which, at intervals, they sally forth to snap up passing insects. They are not so restless as most birds, but sit quite motionless save for an occasional jerk of the tail.

EASTERN KINGBIRD. *Tyrannus tyrannus.*

When this large slaty-black and white Flycatcher flies from one fence-post to another, or from twig to twig, the white band at the tip of its fanlike tail leaves no doubt as to its identity. The red crown-mark, invariably emphasized in color plates, is usually concealed and seldom noticed.

GRAY KINGBIRD. *Tyrannus dominicensis dominicensis.*

The other two Kingbirds have white on the tail; this species has none. Otherwise it resembles the common Kingbird, but is larger, paler, and has the tail slightly forked (Eastern King-bird, rounded). One of the very best characters is the very large bill — a point of distinction that is evident even when the bird is perched at a distance.

ARKANSAS KINGBIRD. *Tyrannus verticalis.*

The best index to the identity of the three Kingbirds is their tails. *The white in this species borders each side of the dark tail as in a Junco or Vesper Sparrow.* The bird is much paler than

the Eastern Kingbird, with *yellowish* under parts, reminding
one of a Crested Flycatcher. The latter species, however, is
a bird of the woods, not the open country that the Kingbirds
prefer.

Each fall, after the common Kingbird has left us, a few
individuals of this Western straggler are reported at scattered
localities along the coast. Some of them even linger into early
winter.

FORKED-TAILED FLYCATCHER. *Muscivora tyrannus.*

A gray-backed Flycatcher with a *black cap* and an *extremely
long forked tail* (much longer than the body). No other North-
American land-bird has a tail at all resembling it, save the
Scissor-tailed Flycatcher. The Scissor-tail is much paler and
whiter, with a *whitish* head and crimson on the sides. The
Fork-tailed Flycatcher is accidental in the United States.

SCISSOR-TAILED FLYCATCHER. *Muscivora forficata.*

See Forked-tailed Flycatcher. Accidental in the Eastern
United States.

NORTHERN CRESTED FLYCATCHER. *Myiarchus crinitus
boreus.*

A large woodland Flycatcher with a *rufous* tail, gray throat
and breast, and yellow belly. No other Flycatcher has a
rufous tail.

SOUTHERN CRESTED FLYCATCHER. *Myiarchus crinitus
crinitus.*

Breeds from coastal Southern South Carolina south through
Florida.

EASTERN PHŒBE. *Sayornis phœbe.*

A Sparrow-sized Flycatcher, gray-brown above and whitish
below, but with *no* conspicuous wing-bars such as the Wood
Pewee and the other small Flycatchers have. This lack of
wing-bars, its well enunciated *phœ-be* call, its upright posture,
and its persistent tail-wagging habit, are all good points. The
bill is *black;* those of the Wood Pewee and the other small
Flycatchers are yellowish or whitish on the lower mandible.

NO EYE-RING
WING-BARS

WOOD PEWEE

NO WING-BARS

PHOEBE

WHITE TUFTS
(NOT ALWAYS VISIBLE)

OLIVE-SIDES

OLIVE-SIDED
FLYCATCHER

LOW BELLY

CRESTED FLYCATCHER

REDDISH TAIL

EYE-RING
WING-BARS

KINGBIRD

WHITE RIM

LEAST FLYCATCHER

THREE OTHER FLYCATCHERS
ARE OF THIS TYPE:
ALDER FLYCATCHER
ACADIAN FLYCATCHER
YELLOW-BELLIED FLYCATCHER

GRAY   COMMON   ARKANSAS

TAILS OF KINGBIRDS

FLYCATCHERS

SAY'S PHŒBE. *Sayornis saya saya.*
Accidental in the East. A large, pale Phœbe with *reddish-ochre* under parts.

LEAST FLYCATCHER. *Empidonax minimus.*
A small Flycatcher, smaller than the Wood Pewee and the Phœbe, with a conspicuous white *eye-ring* and two white *wing-bars.*

The three following species fit the same description exactly; in fact, it is quite risky to attempt to tell them apart by mere variations of color, so closely do they resemble one another. When we chance to be afield during a large 'wave' of these small birds in May, we are forced to let most of them go as 'Empidonax' Flycatchers, but during the breeding-season they are comparatively simple to analyze: their calls are at once characteristic, and their haunts are a clue.

The Least Flycatcher is grayer above and whiter below than the other three, a comparative characteristic which has little value for field recognition. Its song, a sharply snapped *che-bec* with the accent on the *last* syllable, and the orchards and open woodlands which it inhabits, identify it.

YELLOW-BELLIED FLYCATCHER. *Empidonax flaviventris.*
The decidedly yellowish under parts simplify our difficulties with this *Empidonax.* Others of the genus have a tinge of yellow beneath, especially in the fall, but none of the rest has the yellow on the throat.

Its home is the evergreen forest; its call, a simple *per-wee,* a little like a Wood Pewee, but sometimes even more suggestive of the plaintive note of the Semipalmated Plover.

ACADIAN FLYCATCHER. *Empidonax virescens.*
A bird of deciduous woodlands; the *greenest* of all the *Empidonaces.* Its common note is a single *peet;* its call may be rendered *swee'-up* with the accent on the *first* syllable.

ALDER FLYCATCHER. *Empidonax trailli trailli.*
The brownest member of the genus; it is a bit larger and has a whiter throat than the others. It is most likely to be mistaken for the Acadian Flycatcher, but inhabits slashings and

willow and alder thickets at the edges of streams and swamps.

A glance at the voice-descriptions of this species in our standard works will show a great variety of interpretation. One thing is certain — the bird utters quite a different call in Ohio than it does in New York and eastward. In the latter State its call may be rendered *way-be'-o* with the accent on the *middle* syllable. The Ohio birds give utterance to a sneezy *fitz-bew*, as distinctly different from the call of the more eastern birds as that of any two others of the genus. Possibly collecting would prove that other differences existed. The common note is a low *pep*.

EASTERN WOOD PEWEE. *Myiochanes virens.*

A Sparrow-sized Flycatcher, dusky olive-brown above and whitish below. It is most like the Phœbe, but has *two conspicuous wing-bars* and does not wag its tail. The lower mandible of the bill is *yellow*. It does not have the conspicuous eye-ring of the smaller and paler *Empidonax* Flycatchers. Another point, if it be needed, is the wing, which is much longer than that of the Phœbe or the other small Flycatchers, reaching half-way down the tail.

Its call, a drawling, whistled *pee-a-wee*, issuing from the woodland, is characteristic. (The Starling often imitates this note.)

OLIVE-SIDED FLYCATCHER. *Nuttallornis mesoleucus.*

A rather large, bull-headed Flycatcher, usually seen perched at the extreme tip of a dead tree overlooking some brushy slashing. The distinctive points are its large bill, the *dark chest-patches* separated by a narrow strip of white down the center, and two tufts of white which sometimes poke out from behind the wings near the back.

LARKS: ALAUDIDÆ

NORTHERN HORNED LARK. *Otocoris alpestris alpestris.*

A streaked brown terrestrial bird, larger than a Sparrow and smaller than a Robin, with two small erectile black *horns*, and a black collar, or ring, below the yellow throat; *walks*, does not hop; frequents extensive fields and shores; flying overhead, looks like a light-bellied bird with a contrasting *black* tail.

PRAIRIE HORNED LARK. *Otocoris alpestris praticola.*
Like the Horned Lark, but *paler* above, not so pinkish-brown; line over the eye *white*, not yellow; throat white or whitish, but in some individuals faintly tinged with yellow — then the color of the eye-stripe is the surest mark.

HOYT'S HORNED LARK. *Otocoris alpestris hoyti.*
Not certainly separable in the field from the other two.

a. HORNED LARK   *b.* AMERICAN PIPIT

SWALLOWS: HIRUNDINIDÆ

Sparrow-sized birds with long, slim wings and extremely graceful flight.

BAHAMA SWALLOW. *Callichelidon cyaneoviridis.*
Occasional in the southern extremity of Florida; like a small Tree Swallow, steely green above and white below, but with a much more deeply forked, Barn-Swallow-like tail (forked about one inch of its length).

TREE SWALLOW. *Iridoprocne bicolor.*
Steely blue-black or green-black above and *clear white* below; no other Swallow possesses such immaculate white under parts. (See Rough-winged Swallow.)

BANK SWALLOW. *Riparia riparia riparia.*
A small *brown-backed* Swallow with a distinct dark *band*

across the white breast. Our only other brown-backed Swallow, the Rough-wing, lacks this band.

Rough-winged Swallow. *Stelgidopteryx ruficollis serripennis.*

A *brown-backed* Swallow, larger, and lighter brown than the Bank Swallow, with the dark breast-band absent. The whitish under parts shade into a dingy color toward the throat.

Immature Tree Swallows in late summer are rather brownish above and might be mistaken for this species, except for their more snowy-white under parts. The breast of the Rough-wing is dingier; the back browner, not so sooty.

Barn Swallow. *Hirundo erythrogaster.*

Pinkish or cinnamon-buff below, with a *very deeply forked* tail; the only native Swallow that is really 'Swallow-tailed.'

Northern Cliff Swallow. *Petrochelidon albifrons albifrons.*

In flight the *buffy* rump quickly distinguishes the bird; perched overhead with other Swallows, it appears *square-tailed* with a *dark* throat patch.

Purple Martin. *Progne subis subis.*

Our largest Swallow; about eight inches in length. The male is uniformly blue-black *above and below* (no other swallow is black-bellied). The female is whitish-bellied, sometimes with a faint color around the back of the neck; she may be known by her size, and from the much smaller Tree Swallow by the dingy grayness of the throat and breast.

CROWS AND JAYS: CORVIDÆ

Canada Jay. *Perisoreus canadensis canadensis.*

A large *gray* bird of the north woods; larger than a Robin, with a *dark cap* and a white throat; suggests a huge, overgrown Chickadee.

Young birds are dark slate-colored, lightening out towards the tail.

SOLID BLUE-BLACK

GRAYISH BREAST

MALE   PURPLE MARTIN   FEMALE

DEEPLY FORKED TAIL

BUFFY RUMP

BARN SWALLOW   CLIFF SWALLOW

BROWN BACKS

DUSKY THROAT

ROUGH-WINGED SWALLOW

BROWN BREAST BAND

BANK SWALLOW

BLUE-BLACK BACK

TAILLESS APPEARANCE

CLEAR WHITE BREAST

TREE SWALLOW   CHIMNEY SWIFT

Three other forms besides the type are found in Canada:
LABRADOR JAY. *Perisoreus canadensis nigricapillus.* Upper
Ungava and Labrador.

ANTICOSTI JAY. *Perisoreus canadensis barbouri.* Anticosti
Island, Quebec.

NEWFOUNDLAND JAY. *Perisoreus canadensis sanfordi.*
Newfoundland and Nova Scotia.

BLUE JAY. *Cyanocitta cristata cristata.*
The only *large* blue bird, larger than a Robin; blue above,
whitish below, and *crested.* The dissimilar Bluebird is much
smaller, not much larger than a Sparrow, with a *reddish* breast.

FLORIDA BLUE JAY. *Cyanocitta cristata florincola.*
Resident along the Atlantic coast from North Carolina
south to the Everglades and west along the Gulf to Louisiana.

SEMPLE'S BLUE JAY. *Cyanocitta cristata semplei.*
Southern Florida, from the Everglades south.

FLORIDA JAY. *Aphelocoma cærulescens.*
Peninsular Florida. Somewhat similar to the Blue Jay but
slenderer, longer-tailed, and with *no crest.* The wings and tail
are solid blue with no black and white markings.

AMERICAN MAGPIE. *Pica pica hudsonia.*
Accidental in the East. Larger than a Grackle; the only
large *black and white* bird with a long, sweeping tail.

NORTHERN RAVEN. *Corvus corax principalis.*
Although a Raven is nearly twice the size of a Crow, under
certain conditions when comparison is not possible this
difference is deceptive and unreliable. The flight, however, is
distinctive. Hawklike, the Raven alternates flapping with
soaring. It soars on horizontal wings; the Crow and the
Turkey Vulture, with wings bent upward. The ample tail,
seen from below, is distinctly *wedge-shaped.* Perched, at not
too great a distance, the shaggy throat-feathers are evident.
The call is quite different; a Crow caws, a Raven croaks:
cr-r-ruck.

EASTERN CROW. *Corvus brachyrhynchos brachyrhynchos.*
The Crow needs no description.

SOUTHERN CROW. *Corvus brachyrhynchos paulus.*
Smaller and more slender-billed than the Northern sub-species; breeds from Ohio and the lower Potomac, below Washington, south to Florida, where it is replaced by the following form.

FLORIDA CROW. *Corvus brachyrhynchos pascuus.*
Peninsular Florida.

FISH CROW. *Corvus ossifragus.*
A maritime species, seldom found far away from the coast; smaller than the Eastern Crow, safely distinguishable, in the absence of opportunity for comparison, only by voice. The common Crow utters an honest-to-goodness *caw*, the Fish Crow gives a short, nasal *car*. In late spring and summer the voices of young Crows complicate matters. Certain of their calls are almost identical to those of the Fish Crow, but there is a perceptible difference — an indefinable pleading tone that speaks of immaturity.

TITMICE: PARIDÆ

Small gray birds, smaller than Sparrows, with propor-tionately longer tails and small stubby bills; extremely active, hanging upside down as well as right side up in their busy search for insects.

BLACK-CAPPED CHICKADEE. *Penthestes atricapillus atricapil-lus.*
This little fellow so clearly enunciates its own name that there can be no mistake in identity. In the spring he utters another very different call, a two-syllabled whistle: *phœ-be*. The Phœbe Flycatcher does not whistle, but *says* its name simply — *phœbe*.

For beginners we might describe the Chickadee as a small gray and white bird, smaller than a Sparrow, with a *black cap* and a *black bib*.

CAROLINA CHICKADEE. *Penthestes carolinensis carolinensis.*
Nearly identical with the Black-cap, but noticeably smaller, without the conspicuous white created in the wing by the

white feather-edgings. The '*chickadee*' call is higher-pitched and more rapid; the clear two-note whistle of the Black-cap is replaced by a four-syllabled call.

The ranges of the two species are quite distinct. That of the present species is roughly from central New Jersey and central Ohio south.

FLORIDA CHICKADEE. *Penthestes carolinensis impiger.*
The Chickadee of peninsular Florida.

ACADIAN CHICKADEE. *Penthestes hudsonicus littoralis.*
The small size and black bib proclaim it a Chickadee; the general color of the bird is *brown* rather than gray, and it has a *brown cap.*

The notes are slower and more drawling than those of the Black-cap: instead of a lively *chick-a-dee-dee-dee*, it utters a wheezy *chick — che — day —— day.*

HUDSONIAN CHICKADEE. *Penthestes hudsonicus hudsonicus.*
The preceding form is the bird of eastern Canada and the upper edge of the Northeastern States. The present subspecies, which is larger and more rufous, is present from central Ontario westward.

TUFTED TITMOUSE. *Bæolophus bicolor.*
Smaller than a Sparrow; no other small *gray*, mouse-colored bird has a crest.

NUTHATCHES: SITTIDÆ

Small, chubby tree-climbers; smaller than a Sparrow, with a long bill and a stubby tail that is never braced against the tree Woodpecker-like as an aid in climbing. No other tree-climbers ever attempt to go down tree-trunks *head-first*, as these little birds habitually do.

NORTHERN WHITE-BREASTED NUTHATCH. *Sitta carolinensis carolinensis.*
Easily identified by the white breast, the blue-gray back, the black cap, and the habit of frequently traversing tree-trunks *upside down.*

FLORIDA WHITE-BREASTED NUTHATCH. *Sitta carolinensis atkinsi.*

Coastal Georgia, Florida, west along the Gulf Coast to Louisiana, and north in the Mississippi Valley to southern Illinois.

RED-BREASTED NUTHATCH. *Sitta canadensis.*
Smaller than the White-breast; buffier below, with a *broad black line* through the eye.
The call corresponding to the *yank yank* of the White-breast is higher and more nasal, like a 'baby' Nuthatch or a 'tiny tin horn.'

BROWN-HEADED NUTHATCH. *Sitta pusilla pusilla.*
A very small species, smaller than either the Red-breasted or the White-breasted, with a *cinnamon-brown* cap and a conspicuous white spot on the nape of the neck.
GRAY-HEADED NUTHATCH. *Sitta pusilla caniceps.*
The Brown-head of the Florida Peninsula.

CREEPERS: CERTHIIDÆ

BROWN CREEPER. *Certhia familiaris americana.*
Much smaller than a Sparrow; a slim little brown bird with a rather long, stiff tail used as a prop when climbing; often very difficult to detect, so well does the bird blend with the bark of the trees. The name Creeper fits.

WRENS: TROGLODYTIDÆ

Small energetic brown birds, smaller than Sparrows, with slender bills; tails often cocked up over the back.

HOUSE WREN. *Troglodytes aëdon.*
The Wren of the orchards, farmyards, etc.; recognized as a Wren by the small size, brown coloration, energetic actions, and habit of cocking its tail over its back; distinguished from the others by its grayer brown color and the *lack of any evident facial stripings.*

EASTERN WINTER WREN. *Nannus hiemalis hiemalis.*
A very small dark Wren, smaller than a House Wren; has

NO FACIAL STRIPING
GRAY-BROWN ABOVE

SHORT TAIL

DARK BREAST

HOUSE

WINTER

BOLDLY MARKED
OBSCURELY MARKED

WHITISH UNDER-TAIL COVERTS
BROWNISH UNDER-TAIL COVERTS

LONG-BILLED MARSH

SHORT-BILLED MARSH

WHITISH TAIL-TIPS

BRIGHT RUFOUS BACK

CAROLINA

BEWICK'S

WRENS

a much stubbier tail than that species, a light line over the eye and a *dark*, heavily barred belly; often bobs its head; frequents mossy tangles, ravines, brush-piles, etc.

The common note is a two-syllabled *kip-kip*, suggestive in quality of the *chip* of a Song Sparrow.

BEWICK'S WREN. *Thryomanes bewicki bewicki.*
The most characteristic thing about this bird is its long *white-tipped* tail. No other Wren has anything like it. Otherwise, it is somewhat between the Carolina and House Wrens in size and appearance. There are instances where this species has been passed by as a Carolina Wren (because of the white stripe over the eye) until its decidedly Song-Sparrow-like song was heard.

CAROLINA WREN. *Thryothorus ludovicianus ludovicianus.*
The largest and reddest of the Wrens; as large as a small Sparrow; *rufous-red* above and buffy below, with a conspicuous *white stripe* over the eye. The Long-billed Marsh Wren has a white eye-line, but that bird is striped on the back; the Carolina is unmarked. The Bewick's Wren differs in being less rufous, and having white tail-tips.

FLORIDA WREN. *Thryothorus ludovicianus miamensis.*
A larger, darker race of the Carolina Wren; a resident of the Florida Peninsula.

LONG-BILLED MARSH WREN. *Telmatodytes palustris palustris.*
The Wren of the cat-tail marsh; brown with a conspicuous white stripe over the eye; known from the other Wrens with white eye-stripes by the black and white stripes on the back. (Bewick's and Carolina are unmarked above.) The Short-billed Marsh Wren is smaller, without the conspicuous eye-line.

Several forms besides the type are found in the East.

PRAIRIE MARSH WREN. *Telmatodytes palustris dissaëptus.*
Not separable in the field from the preceding. It is better to call them all Long-bills, rather than to attempt any discrimination in the field, even where this subspecies is *supposed* to occur.

WORTHINGTON'S **MARSH** WREN. *Telmatodytes palustris griseus.*

Easily recognized by its *grayness*; breeds along the Atlantic Coast from South Carolina to northern Florida.

MARIAN'S MARSH WREN. *Telmatodytes palustris marianæ.*

A small, dark Marsh Wren; breast *shaded or speckled with drab.* Resident along the Gulf from Mississippi to Old Tampa Bay, Florida.

LOUISIANA MARSH WREN. *Telmatodytes palustris thryophilus.*

Somewhat like *marianæ*, but the breast is not spotted Breeds along the Gulf in Louisiana; winters to the west coast of Florida.

SHORT-BILLED MARSH WREN. *Cistothorus stellaris.*

The Wren of the wet meadows and *grassy* marshes. Very buffy; distinguished from the Long-bill by the less contrastingly marked upper parts, and the lack of a conspicuous white line over the eye; when the tail is cocked over the back, the much browner under tail-coverts are evident.

The Long-bill prefers cat-tails; the present species, wet sedgy meadows or the edges of swamps. The song of the Long-bill is rather liquid; that of the Short-bill, a staccato chattering — *chap... chap... chap. chap. chap. chapper-rrrrr.* The call-note is of the same quality as the song: a single *chap.*

THRASHERS, MOCKINGBIRDS, ETC.: MIMIDÆ

MOCKINGBIRD. *Mimus polyglottos polyglottos.*

As large as a Robin, but more slender; gray above and white below, with large white patches on the wings and tail, conspicuous in flight. Mockingbirds resemble Shrikes somewhat, but lack the black facial masks.

CATBIRD. *Dumetella carolinensis.*

Smaller and slimmer than a Robin; *slaty-gray* with a black cap, and with *chestnut-red* under tail-coverts (these are seldom noticed in the field). The catlike mewing note is distinctive. The only other uniformly gray song-bird, the female Cowbird, is shorter-tailed and stouter-billed, and lacks the reddish under tail-coverts.

BROWN THRASHER. *Toxostoma rufum.*
Slightly larger and slimmer than a Robin; bright *rufous-red* above, heavily striped below. Differs from the Thrushes in possessing a much longer tail and a curved bill and in being *streaked*, rather than spotted, below.

The song resembles the Catbird's, but the Thrasher *repeats* each phrase.

THRUSHES, ROBINS, BLUEBIRDS, ETC.: TURDIDÆ

The five Eastern species that bear the name 'Thrush' are brown-backed birds with *spotted* breasts. Robins and Blue-birds, though entirely unlike the other Thrushes in color, betray definite indications of their relationship to this group through their speckle-breasted young.

EASTERN ROBIN. *Turdus migratorius migratorius.*
The one bird that everybody knows.

VARIED THRUSH. *Ixoreus nævius meruloides.*
Accidental in the East; like a Robin, but with an orange eye-stripe, orange wing-bars, and a black band across the breast.

NORTHERN WOOD THRUSH. *Hylocichla mustelina.*
Smaller than a Robin; bright-brown above; breast and sides heavily spotted; distinguished from the other Thrushes by the deepening redness *about the head* and the larger, more numerous, *round* spots. The Thrasher is larger, much longer-tailed, and *streaked* below, not spotted.

EASTERN HERMIT THRUSH. *Hylocichla guttata faxoni.*
The *reddish tail*, conspicuous as the bird flies away, is the Hermit Thrush's mark. Three of the five Thrushes are tinged with reddish-brown in a greater or less degree: the Veery is uniformly colored above, the Wood Thrush is reddest about the head, and the Hermit reddest on the tail. At rest the

Hermit has a characteristic trick of *raising* the tail slowly at frequent intervals.

The Fox Sparrow is reddish-tailed, but the under parts are very heavily *streaked*, not spotted. The bill of the Sparrow is thick and conical, that of the Thrush, slender.

OLIVE-BACKED THRUSH. *Hylocichla ustulata swainsoni.*

When we come upon a Thrush that lacks any warmth of color in its plumage and is uniformly gray-brown or olive-brown above, then we can be sure we have found one of two species. If the bird possesses a conspicuous buffy *eye-ring* and *buffy cheeks*, it is the Olive-backed Thrush; if the cheeks are gray and the eye-ring indistinct or lacking, then it is the Gray-cheek.

GRAY-CHEEKED THRUSH. *Hylocichla minima aliciæ.*

Like the Olive-back, this species is an olive-brown, or gray-brown, Thrush. As its name implies it is gray-cheeked, not buffy-cheeked like the other bird, and lacks the conspicuous buffy eye-ring.

BICKNELL'S THRUSH. *Hylocichla minima minima.*

Similar to the preceding form, but much smaller. Gray-cheeked Thrushes *breeding* within the limits of the United States, or in Nova Scotia, are of this subspecies.

VEERY. *Hylocichla fuscescens.*

A Thrush *uniformly* cinnamon-brown or tawny-brown above is quite certainly a Veery. (Gray-cheek and Olive-back are dull *gray-brown* above; Wood Thrush is red about the head; Hermit, reddish on the tail.) Of all the Thrushes this is the least spotted; at a distance the bird appears quite clear-breasted.

EASTERN BLUEBIRD. *Sialia sialis sialis.*

A little larger than a Sparrow; the only blue bird with a *red* breast (Blue Jay has white breast; Indigo Bunting, blue breast); appears round-shouldered when perching.

Young Bluebirds are speckle-breasted, devoid of red, but there is always a considerable amount of telltale blue in the wings and tail.

REDDISH HEAD

REDDISH TAIL

ARGE
UND SPOTS

WOOD

HERMIT

UNIFORMLY REDDISH
UPPERPARTS

VERY LITTLE
SPOTTING

VEERY

GRAY CHEEKS

EYE-RING
BUFFY CHEEKS

UNIFORMLY GRAY-BROWN
UPPERPARTS

GRAY-CHEEKED

OLIVE-BACKED

THRUSHES

GREENLAND WHEATEAR. *Œnanthe œnanthe leucorhoa.*
Accidental in the eastern United States; a ground bird of
the open country, barrens, etc.; shaped a little like a Bluebird,
but smaller. In winter plumage, both adults and young are
olive-brown above with light cinnamon-brown under parts
and blackish wings. It is best recognized by its *white rump
and sides of tail* contrasting with the *black central feathers and
terminal band* of the latter (the black appears like an inverted
T superimposed on the white).

TOWNSEND'S SOLITAIRE. *Myadestes townsendi.*
Accidental in the East; slightly smaller and slimmer than
a Robin; uniformly gray with a narrow white eye-ring and
white outer tail-feathers, like a Junco; could be confused with
a Catbird, except for the white in the tail and lack of chestnut
under tail-coverts. The Arkansas Kingbird possesses a
similarly patterned tail, and both birds act like Flycatchers,
but the Kingbird is yellow below, not gray.

KINGLETS AND GNATCATCHERS: SYLVIIDÆ

BLUE-GRAY GNATCATCHER. *Polioptila cærulea cærulea.*
Gnatcatchers remind one a little of miniature Mockingbirds
in color and actions. They are very tiny, slender mites,
smaller even than Chickadees, blue-gray above and whitish
below, with a white eye-ring and a *long, contrastingly colored
tail* (black in the center, white on the sides). The Cerulean
Warbler might be mistaken for it, but that bird is shorter-
tailed, lacks the eye-ring, and has a *narrow black ring* across
the breast.

GOLDEN-CROWNED KINGLET. *Regulus satrapa satrapa.*
Kinglets are tiny mites of birds, half the size of Sparrows.
Their diminutive proportions and somber olive-gray backs
make them difficult to discern among the thick branches of the
evergreens through which they forage. Were it not for their
fidgetiness, it might be like looking for the proverbial needle
in the haystack.
The present species at all times shows a conspicuous bright

crown, yellow in the female, orange in the male. Another point of distinction (if it be needed) is that the Golden-crown has a *white stripe* over the eye, the Ruby-crown a white eye-ring.

The call-note is a high, wiry *tee-tee-tee*. The Ruby-crown utters a husky two-syllabled *zĭ-da*.

EASTERN RUBY-CROWNED KINGLET. *Corthylio calendula calendula.*
Very tiny and short-tailed; olive-gray above with two pale wing-bars; male with a *scarlet* crown-patch (usually concealed). The best recognition mark is the conspicuous *white eye-ring*, which gives the bird a big-eyed appearance. Any Kinglet not showing a conspicuous crown-patch is of this species. The stubby tail separates it at once from any of the Warblers.

WAGTAILS AND PIPITS: MOTACILLIDÆ

AMERICAN PIPIT. *Anthus spinoletta rubescens.*
Near the size of a Sparrow, but with a *slender* bill; under parts *buffy* with streakings; *outer tail-feathers white;* frequents plowed fields, shore flats, etc. It may be known from the Vesper Sparrow, which also shows white outer tail-feathers, by the buffy under parts and the habits of *constantly wagging its tail*, of *walking* instead of hopping, and of dipping up and down when in flight. (See cut, page 99.)

SPRAGUE'S PIPIT. *Anthus spraguei.*
Occasional in the Southern States in winter. Whiter below than the American Pipit and said not to wag its tail.

WAXWINGS: BOMBYCILLIDÆ

BOHEMIAN WAXWING. *Bombycilla garrula pallidiceps.*
The Cedar-bird is the common Waxwing; the Bohemian Waxwing, the wanderer, occurs but rarely, or at erratic intervals, chiefly in winter. It resembles the common bird closely, but is larger, has some *white in the wing*, is gray rather than brown, and possesses *chestnut-red* under tail-coverts instead of white.

CEDAR WAXWING. *Bombycilla cedrorum.*

Between the size of a Sparrow and a Robin; a sleek, *crested,* brown bird with a broad *yellow* band at the tip of the tail. It is our only *brown* bird with a long crest.

a. CEDAR WAXWING   *b.* BOHEMIAN WAXWING

SHRIKES: LANIIDÆ

NORTHERN SHRIKE. *Lanius borealis borealis.*

If in the Northern States during the winter months we see a Robin-sized bird, sitting quite still, *alone* in the *tip-top* of some tree, we are quite certainly looking at a Northern Shrike. Closer inspection shows it to be light gray above and white below, with a *black mask* through the eyes. On taking flight it drops low, and, progressing with a peculiar easy wing-motion on a bee-line course, rises suddenly to its tree-top perch.

This species can be told from the very similar Migrant Shrike by its slightly larger size and *finely-barred* breast. Another very good point, but one that requires close scrutiny, is the bill: that of the Migrant is solid black; the basal portion of the lower mandible of the present species is *pale flesh-colored.* The Migrant has a narrow strip of black above the bill. Generally speaking, however, winter Shrikes in the North are Northerns, and summer Shrikes, Migrants, but there are times during the year when both might be expected to occur.

Young birds are browner but still recognizable as this species by the fine vermiculations on the breast.

MIGRANT SHRIKE. *Lanius ludovicianus migrans.*

Slightly smaller than a Robin; big-headed and slim-tailed; gray above and white below, with a conspicuous *black mask* through the eyes. (See Northern Shrike.)

LOGGERHEAD SHRIKE. *Lanius ludovicianus ludovicianus.*

Similar to the preceding; occurs along the Atlantic coast from southern North Carolina to southern Florida and west along the Gulf to Louisiana. The Mockingbird bears a certain resemblance, but has more white in the wings and lacks the black mask.

STARLINGS: STURNIDÆ

STARLING. *Sturnus vulgaris vulgaris.*

The Starling, like the Crow, English Sparrow, and Robin, should be one of the few birds that needs no introduction at all, yet it is surprising how often someone will venture to ask what bird it is that has a long yellow bill and looks like a Blackbird. Then again, someone who already knows the Starling, having seen it in flocks at a little distance, will come in with the description of a remarkable bird, glossed all over with purple and green, and sprinkled with tiny white specks. They are rather chagrined when they are told that their 'unusual bird' is a Starling. The truth is that they never examined one closely before.

The Starling is the *short-tailed* 'Blackbird'; the Grackle, the long-tailed; and the Red-wing, Rusty, and Cowbird are the happy mediums.

In the winter plumage the Starling is heavily speckled. The bill is dark, changing to yellow as spring approaches. No other 'Blackbird' has a *yellow* bill.

Young birds are dark dusky gray, a little like the female Cowbird, but the tail is shorter, and the bill longer and more spike-like, not stout and conical.

The male Starling sings from the tree-top, house-gutter, or chimney; many of the notes are extremely musical; others harsh; and many of them are very good imitations of other species. He is a most adept mocker.

VIREOS: VIREONIDÆ

Small olive-backed birds, slightly smaller than most Sparrows; very much like the Warblers, but with somewhat heavier bills and less active, slowly searching for insects under the leaves instead of flitting about.

Of the six commonest Eastern species, three — the Yellow-throated, Blue-headed, and White-eyed Vireos — have white wing-bars; the Philadelphia, Warbling, and Red-eyed have none. This is a helpful thing to remember, as the rest of the identification becomes easier through elimination.

WHITE-EYED VIREO. *Vireo griseus griseus.*

A small Vireo of the shrubbery and undergrowth; yellow-green, with wing-bars, yellowish sides, and *white eyes.* Two other common Vireos — the Yellow-throated and Blue-headed — possess wing-bars. The *bright-yellow* throat and breast identify the Yellow-throat; the *snow-white* throat and breast, the Blue-head. If the bird has neither, but is washed beneath with a dingy yellow, then it is this species.

Because of its size and markings the bird can be easily mistaken for one of the small Flycatchers. Even the song is more like that of a Flycatcher than a Vireo — a sharply enunciated *chick'-per-whee-oo-chick'.*

KEY WEST VIREO. *Vireo griseus maynardi.*

The White-eye of the Florida Keys.

BERMUDA VIREO. *Vireo griseus bermudianus.*

The Bermuda form.

BELL'S VIREO. *Vireo belli belli.*

Breeds east to Illinois and northwestern Indiana. A small olive-green Vireo with wing-bars and a pale yellowish-washed breast; resembles the White-eye but has *dark* eyes and lacks the yellow 'spectacles.' The presence of wing-bars distinguishes it from the Warbling Vireo.

YELLOW-THROATED VIREO. *Vireo flavifrons.*

Olive-green above, with white wing-bars and a *bright yellow* throat and breast. It is the only Vireo possessing any *bright* yellow. The similarly colored Yellow-breasted Chat is larger and has no wing-bars.

BLUE-HEADED VIREO. *Vireo solitarius solitarius.*

A Vireo with white wing-bars; differentiated from the other two possessing wing-bars — the Yellow-throated and the White-eye — by the *blue-gray* head, *white eye-ring,* and *snowy-white* throat.

MOUNTAIN VIREO. *Vireo solitarius alticola.*

This form of the Blue-head breeds in the Alleghenies from Maryland to northern Georgia.

BLACK-WHISKERED VIREO. *Vireo calidris barbatulus.*

A summer resident of the southern extremity of Florida and the Keys; resembles the Red-eyed Vireo, but has a narrow black streak, or 'whisker' mark, on each side of the throat.

RED-EYED VIREO. *Vireo olivaceus.*

A Vireo *without* wing-bars; olive-green above, white below; best characterized by the gray cap and the *black-bordered white stripe* over the eye. The red eye is of little aid in identification. The Warbling Vireo is paler, without such contrasting facial striping.

PHILADELPHIA VIREO. *Vireo philadelphicus.*

The only Vireo that combines the characters of *unbarred* wings and *yellowish under parts.* The similarly patterned Warbling Vireo, aside from lacking the yellow, is paler-backed, not so olive. Here it might be mentioned that though it looks more like the Warbling Vireo, it sings more like the Red-eye.

The Orange-crowned Warbler is very similar, but the more restless, Warbler-like actions and the *faint dusky streaks* on the breast identify it. The fall Tennessee Warbler is also similar but has *clear-white* under tail-coverts. At this point it might be added that anyone unable to tell a Vireo from a Warbler is hardly qualified to recognize this species. A Vireo is always chubbier and less active. The bill is stouter, less needle-like.

EASTERN WARBLING VIREO. *Vireo gilvus gilvus.*

Three species of Vireos have *no* wing-bars. If the head is contrastingly striped, it is a Red-eye. If the head is *indistinctly* striped and the under parts are *white*, then it is the

YELLOW-THROATED

~~~T YELLOW
~~~BREAST

PHILADELPHIA

INDISTINCT
EYE-STRIPES

YELLOWISH
UNDERPARTS

BLUE-HEADED

WHITE EYE-RING
BLUISH HEAD

WARBLING

INDISTINCT
EYE-STRIPES

WHITISH
UNDERPARTS

WHITE-EYED

WHITE EYE

RED-EYED

GRAY CAP
BLACK AND WHITE
LINES OVER EYE

WITH WING-BARS

WITHOUT WING-BARS

VIREOS

present species. The Philadelphia Vireo is darker and more olive above and yellowish below.

The song of this species is a rather lengthy languid warble much unlike the abrupt phraseology of the other Vireos. It sounds a little like the Purple Finch's song.

HONEY CREEPERS: CŒREBIDÆ

BAHAMA HONEY CREEPER. *Cœreba bahamensis.*
Accidental in southern Florida; about the size of a House Wren, or near five inches; bill *decurved;* easily recognized by its *black, yellow, and white* coloration. The upper parts are black, the breast and rump yellow, and the belly and line over the eye white.

WOOD WARBLERS: COMPSOTHLYPIDÆ

These are the sprightly 'butterflies' of the bird world — bright-colored mites, smaller than Sparrows. The Vireos are similar, but their movements when patiently foraging among the leaves and twigs are rather sluggish, unlike the active flittings of the Warblers.

In the fall of the year there is a preponderance of olive-yellow species — adults that have changed their plumage, immature birds, etc. The list below, of the more nondescript species that at that time of the year are more or less olive-colored above and yellowish on the under parts, devoid of obviously distinctive markings, may be of assistance in running them down.

Species with wing-bars:

Magnolia
Bay-breasted
Black-poll
Pine
Black-throated Green (young female)

Species without wing-bars:

Tennessee
Nashville
Orange-crowned

> Mourning (young)
> Connecticut (female and young)
> Maryland Yellow-throat (female and young)
> Hooded (female and young)
> Wilson's (female and young)
> Bachman's (female; southern United States)

BLACK AND WHITE WARBLER. *Mniotilta varia.*

The most distinctively-marked of the group; *striped lengthwise with black and white* — the zebra's counterpart among birds; *creeps* along tree-trunks and branches.

The Black-poll Warbler is the only one that at all resembles it, but that species has a *solid black cap.*

PROTHONOTARY WARBLER. *Protonotaria citrea.*

Entire head and breast *deep yellow,* almost orange; wings *blue-gray;* sexes similar. Frequents wooded swamps.

It is a toss-up between the Yellow Warbler and the Blue-wing for the distinction of being the species most often misidentified by the hopeful beginner as this rarer bird. The Yellow Warbler has *yellowish* wings; the Blue-wing, *white wing-bars* and a black mark through the eye.

SWAINSON'S WARBLER. *Limnothlypis swainsoni.*

The rank, tangled swamps of the South are the home of the Swainson's Warbler. Both sexes are quite plain; *olive-brown* above and dingy white below, with a conspicuous *whitish stripe* over the eye.

The Worm-eating Warbler differs in having *black stripes* on the crown; the Water-thrush, in possessing heavily *streaked* under parts.

WORM-EATING WARBLER. *Helmitheros vermivorus.*

Dull olive-green, with *black stripes* on the top of the head. Chiefly a ground bird, inhabiting woodland hillsides, ravines, etc.; in this sort of territory (where the bird occurs) a Chipping-Sparrow-like trill can almost invariably be traced to this species.

GOLDEN-WINGED WARBLER. *Vermivora chrysoptera.*

Gray above and white below, with a yellow forehead patch,

broad yellow wing-patch, black patch through eye, and black throat. No other Warbler has the combined characters of *yellow wing-patch and black throat*. Females resemble the males, but are duller, the black being largely replaced by gray.

The song is unlike that of any other Warbler, except the Blue-wing — *beee-bzz-bzz-bzz*. The Blue-wing sounds much the same but usually has but one buzz — *beee-bzzz*.

BLUE-WINGED WARBLER. *Vermivora pinus.*

Face and under parts yellow; *black mark through eye;* wings with two broad *white* bars. The narrow black eye-mark distinguishes it from any other largely yellowish Warbler (Yellow Warbler, Prothonotary, etc.).

BREWSTER'S WARBLER. *Vermivora leucobronchialis.*

The Golden-winged and Blue-winged Warblers are our only song-birds which commonly hybridize. Two distinct types are produced, the Lawrence's Warbler and the present bird, which occurs the more commonly of the two. Typical Brewster's are like Golden-wings without the black throat, or, putting it differently, like Blue-wings with whitish under parts. There is a good deal of variation; some individuals have white wing-bars, others yellow, and some birds are tinged with yellow below. The thin black eye-mark, as in the Blue-wing, and the white or largely white, instead of solid yellow, under parts are diagnostic. The most outstanding factor to consider between the two hybrids is the black throat, which the Lawrence must have and the Brewster's must lack.

LAWRENCE'S WARBLER. *Vermivora lawrencei.*

Largely yellowish with white wing-bars, like a Blue-wing, but with the wide black eye-patch and black throat of the Golden-wing. It is the only yellow-breasted Warbler with a black throat-patch (except Bachman's Warbler of the southern United States). Most examples of this rare hybrid conform pretty closely with the type.

BACHMAN'S WARBLER. *Vermivora bachmani.*

Breeds in the Southern States in tangled, thicket-grown swamps such as the Swainson's Warbler frequents.

Male: — Olive-green above; face and under parts yellow; *throat-patch and crown-patch black.* The only other Warbler with the combined characters of black throat-patch and yellow under parts is the Lawrence's Warbler, which has two broad *white wing-bars,* a broad black patch through the eye, and *none* on the crown. In the Hooded Warbler the black completely encircles the neck.

Female: — Similar to the male; upper parts olive-green; front of face and under parts yellow; crown grayish. There are two other Warblers without wing-bars that are solid yellow below and olive-green above — the female Hooded and the female Wilson's. Neither of them has the well-marked contrast of *yellow forehead* and blue-gray crown. The yellowish bend in the wing is also an aid.

TENNESSEE WARBLER. *Vermivora peregrina.*

Adult male in spring: — Very plain, unmarked save for a *conspicuous white stripe over the eye;* head gray, contrasting with olive-green back; under parts white. The bird in this plumage, with the white eye-stripe, is much like the Red-eyed and the Philadelphia Vireos, but the smaller size, the Warbler actions, and the thin, fine-pointed bill identify it.

Adult female in spring: — Similar to the male, but head less gray and under parts slightly yellowish. The eye-line is the best mark.

Adults and immature in autumn: — Olive-green above, yellowish below; the only Warbler with the combined characters of *unstreaked* yellowish breast and *conspicuous* yellowish line over the eye. The Orange-crowned Warbler is somewhat similar to autumn birds, but the breast is faintly streaked and the under tail-coverts are *yellow,* not white as in the Tennessee.

ORANGE-CROWNED WARBLER. *Vermivora celata celata.*

A dull-colored Warbler *without* wing-bars; olive-green above, dingy yellow below; *under parts faintly streaked;* 'orange crown' seldom visible (Nashville also has a veiled crown-patch); sexes similar.

The points to remember are the faint, blurry streakings and the lack of wing-bars.

In the *autumn immature,* the plumage most frequently

WARBLERS (I)

1. KENTUCKY WARBLER, MALE

2. MOURNING WARBLER, *a*. MALE; *b*. FEMALE

3. CONNECTICUT WARBLER, *a*. MALE; *b*. FEMALE

4. NASHVILLE WARBLER

5. NORTHERN YELLOW-THROAT, *a*. MALE; *b*. FEMALE

6. HOODED WARBLER, *a*. MALE; *b*. FEMALE

7. WILSON'S WARBLER, *a*. MALE; *b*. FEMALE

8. BACHMAN'S WARBLER, *a*. MALE; *b*. FEMALE

9. BLUE-WINGED WARBLER, MALE

10. BREWSTER'S WARBLER

11. GOLDEN-WINGED WARBLER, MALE

12. LAWRENCE'S WARBLER

13. PROTHONOTARY WARBLER, *a*. MALE; *b*. FEMALE

14. YELLOW-BREASTED CHAT

15. YELLOW WARBLER, *a*. MALE; *b*. FEMALE

16. ORANGE-CROWNED WARBLER

17. WORM-EATING WARBLER

18. SWAINSON'S WARBLER

19. TENNESSEE WARBLER, MALE

20. PARULA WARBLER, *a*. MALE; *b*. FEMALE

21. BLACK-THROATED BLUE WARBLER, *a*. MALE; *b*. FEMALE

22. CERULEAN WARBLER, *a*. MALE; *b*. FEMALE

observed in the Northeast, the bird is greenish drab throughout — barely perceptibly paler on the under parts. Other
similar birds are the autumn Tennessee Warbler, which lacks
the faint breast-streakings and has *white* under tail-coverts,
not yellow, and the Philadelphia Vireo, which has a light
stripe over the eye and lacks the streakings. The Vireo is
sluggish; the Warbler, active.

NASHVILLE WARBLER. *Vermivora ruficapilla ruficapilla.*
A small, rather plain Warbler; throat and under parts
bright yellow; head gray, contrasting with the olive-green
back; eye-ring white; sexes similar.
The *white eye-ring* in conjunction with the *yellow* throat is
the best mark. The Connecticut Warbler has a white eye-ring,
but its throat is gray.

NORTHERN PARULA WARBLER. *Compsothlypis americana
pusilla.*
Male: — The only *bluish* Warbler with a *yellow* throat and
breast. Two broad white wing-bars are also conspicuous.
A suffused yellowish patch on the back is a clinching point,
but as Parulas usually range high, it is not often that we are
able to see that feature. The most useful field mark of all, one
that is visible from below, is a *dark band* crossing the yellow
of the breast.
Female: — Similar, but with the breast band indistinct or
lacking. The general blue and yellow color is distinctive.
SOUTHERN PARULA WARBLER. *Compsothlypis americana
americana.* Breeds from Washington, D.C., south to Florida.
Breeding birds in the lower Mississippi valley are of the
preceding race.

YELLOW WARBLER. *Dendroica æstiva æstiva.*
The only small bird that in the field appears to be *all yellow.*
Many of the other Warblers are yellow below, but none of
them is as yellow on the back, wings, and tail. Many Warblers
have white spots in the tail; this is the only species with *yellow*
spots. At close range the male shows chestnut-red breast-
streakings. In the female these are faint or lacking.
The Goldfinch shares the nickname 'Yellow-bird,' but has
black wings and a *black* tail.

MAGNOLIA WARBLER. *Dendroica magnolia.*

The Magnolia's former name, 'Black and Yellow Warbler,' well describes it. The upper parts are largely blackish, with large white patches on the wings and tail; the under parts yellow with heavy black stripings.

Three other Warblers with bright yellow under parts are striped with black beneath — the Canada, Cape May, and Prairie — but none of them has the black and white coloration of the upper plumage. From below, when the upper plumage is not visible, the tail of the Magnolia Warbler appears white with a *wide black terminal band.*

In the *fall* Magnolias are quite brown above and yellow below, the black stripings reduced to a few sparse marks on the flanks. The contrasting *yellow rump* will then separate it from any other species except the Myrtle and the Cape May. The black tail, crossed midway by a very broad white band, as in spring, eliminates those two.

CAPE MAY WARBLER. *Dendroica tigrina.*

Male: — Patterned tiger-like; under parts yellow narrowly striped, with black; rump yellow; crown black; cheek-patch chestnut; *the only Warbler with chestnut cheeks.*

Females and immature birds lack the chestnut cheeks and are duller, but retain enough of the male's striped pattern to be recognizable.

Juvenile females are especially nondescript; the breast is almost white, the streakings narrow (a little like a female Myrtle, without the yellow areas). A good point, if it can be observed, is a dim, suffused patch of yellow behind the ear.

BLACK-THROATED BLUE WARBLER. *Dendroica cærulescens cærulescens.*

Male: — Very clean-cut; *blue, black, and white;* upper parts blue-gray; throat and sides black; breast and belly white.

Females and young are very plain little birds, olive-backed, with a narrow white line over the eye and a small *white wing-spot.*

CAIRNS'S WARBLER. *Dendroica cærulescens cairnsi.*

Similar to the preceding, but the male has the back spotted with black. Some individuals of *D. c. cærulescens* are very similarly marked, however, so there can be no definite discrimination in the field. The present form is the southern race, breeding in the Alleghenies from Maryland to Georgia.

MYRTLE WARBLER. *Dendroica coronata.*
The Myrtle Warbler can be identified in any plumage by its *yellow rump*, which, in conjunction with its note, a loud *check*, is unmistakable.
Male in spring: — Blue-gray above; white below, with a heavy inverted U of black on the breast and sides, and a patch of yellow on the crown and one on each side.
Female in spring: — Brown instead of bluish, but pattern similar.
Winter adults and young: — Brownish above; white below, streaked with dark; rump yellow.
The white throat and under parts distinguish the Myrtle from the Cape May and Magnolia Warblers, the only other species that possess contrasting yellow rump-patches.

AUDUBON'S WARBLER. *Dendroica auduboni auduboni.*
Accidental in the East; like the Myrtle Warbler but in adults with a *yellow* instead of white throat.

BLACK-THROATED GRAY WARBLER. *Dendroica nigrescens.*
Accidental in the East; gray above and white below; *black crown, black patch through eye, and black patch on throat;* most like the Black-poll Warbler, which lacks the black eye- and throat-patches. The Golden-wing might possibly be transformed into this rarity by the hopeful enthusiast, but that bird has a *yellow* crown and a large yellow wing-patch.
Females lack the black throat but retain the black eye- and crown-patches. In no plumage would the bird possess the white cheeks of the Black-poll.

BLACK-THROATED GREEN WARBLER. *Dendroica virens virens.*
Male: — The bright *yellow face* framed by the *black throat* and olive-green crown and back is the best mark.
Female: — Recognized by its yellow face-patch, but with much less black on the throat and under parts.

Young female in autumn: — Under parts yellowish; no black on the throat and upper breast; somewhat like a Pine Warbler, but with brighter yellow cheeks.

WAYNE'S WARBLER. *Dendroica virens waynei.*
An isolated race of the Black-throated Green Warbler, found breeding locally in the large swamps of the South Carolina coastal district.

CERULEAN WARBLER. *Dendroica cerulea.*
Male: — Blue above, white below. *A narrow black ring* crossing the upper breast is the best mark when the bird is high overhead. No other white-breasted Warbler is so marked.
Female: — Blue-gray and olive-green above and whitish below, with two white wing-bars and a white line over the eye. The Tennessee Warbler is somewhat similar but lacks the white wing-bars. The Cerulean resembles even more closely the autumn Black-poll but is greener above and whiter below.

BLACKBURNIAN WARBLER. *Dendroica fusca.*
Male in spring: — Black and white with much bright *fiery orange* about the head and throat; unmistakable. The differently patterned Redstart is the only other small bird of similar color.
Female: — Paler, but still orange enough on the throat to be recognized as a Blackburnian.
Autumn birds: — Color-pattern similar, but paler, the orange more yellowish. The clean-cut yellow head-stripings are distinctive.

YELLOW-THROATED WARBLER. *Dendroica dominica dominica.*
A gray-backed Warbler with a yellow throat. Under parts white; two white wing-bars; white line over the eye and black stripes on the sides; creeps about the branches of trees in the manner of a Black and White Warbler.
The female Blackburnian is slightly similar but is not so white below and is *broadly striped with yellow* over the eye and through the center of the crown. The present species appears to be yellow on the throat only.

SYCAMORE WARBLER. *Dendroica dominica albilora.*

Almost identical with the preceding, from which it might be distinguished at extremely short range by the lack of any yellow between the eye and the bill. The eye-stripe is entirely white.

The Yellow-throated Warbler is the coastal bird; west of the Alleghenies its place is taken by the present race.

CHESTNUT-SIDED WARBLER. *Dendroica pensylvanica.*

Adults in spring: — Easily identified by the *yellow* crown and the *chestnut* sides. The only other bird with chestnut sides, the Bay-breast, has a chestnut throat and a dark crown, thus appearing quite dark-headed.

Autumn birds are quite different — greenish above and white below, with a white eye-ring and two wing-bars. Adults usually retain some of the chestnut. The lemon-colored shade of green, in connection with the white under parts is sufficient for recognition.

BAY-BREASTED WARBLER. *Dendroica castanea.*

Male in spring: — A dark-looking Warbler with *chestnut throat, upper breast, and sides,* and a large spot of pale buff on the side of the neck. The Chestnut-sided Warbler is much lighter-colored, with a *white* throat and yellow crown.

Female in spring: — Similar in pattern to the male, but dimmer and more indistinctly marked.

Autumn birds: — Totally different; olive-green above with two white wing-bars, dingy buffy-yellow below. Some individuals have traces of bay on the sides. The fall Black-poll is very similar but has more distinct streakings on the sides and *white* under tail-coverts instead of yellow.

BLACK-POLL WARBLER. *Dendroica striata.*

Male in spring: — A striped gray Warbler with a *solid black cap;* reminds the beginner of a Chickadee, but lacks the black throat. The Black and White Warbler, the only other species with which it might be confused, has a *striped* crown.

Female in spring: — Less heavily streaked, lacking the black crown-patch; a plain, black-streaked Warbler, greenish-gray above, white below; may be known from the Black and

White by the lack of contrasting head-stripings, and from the female Myrtle by the absence of yellow in the plumage.

Autumn birds: — Olive-green above, with two white wing-bars; dingy yellow below, faintly streaked. This is the common greenish-looking fall Warbler with white wing-bars, the one which causes the field student so much trouble. (See Bay-breasted Warbler (fall) and Pine Warbler.)

NORTHERN PINE WARBLER. *Dendroica pinus pinus.*
Frequents coniferous woods, especially groves of pitch pines.

Male: — Olive-green above with two white wing-bars; under parts canary yellow, brightest on the throat; breast dimly streaked. No other *bright* yellow-breasted Warbler, without other conspicuous field marks, has white wing-bars. The Yellow-throated Vireo is quite similar, but does not show the faint breast streaks or the white spots in the tail as in the present species.

Female and immature: — Very nondescript; dull olive above, with *two white wing-bars;* under parts whitish or dull yellow, faintly streaked with dusky along the sides; best identified by the 'boiling-down' system of elimination.

Autumn Black-polls and Bay-breasts are very similar — dingy, olive-colored Warblers with white wing-bars. The plain, *unstreaked* back of the Pine Warbler, if it can be seen, at once eliminates either of those two. In addition, the Bay-breast would have yellow under tail-coverts, not white.

FLORIDA PINE WARBLER. *Dendroica pinus florida.*
Resident in southern Florida, south of the latitude 29° (Volusia, Lake, and Citrus Counties).

KIRTLAND'S WARBLER. *Dendroica kirtlandi.*
Confined as a breeder to Oscoda, Crawford, and Roscommon Counties, Michigan. Rather large for a Warbler; gray above and yellow below, with some large sparse spotting on the breast and sides; sexes similar.

The bird *wags* its tail much like a Palm Warbler; no other *gray-backed* Warbler has this habit. Aside from the habit of tail-wagging, the bird may be known from the Canada Warbler, which is also gray above and yellow below, by the

WARBLERS (II)

1. YELLOW-THROATED WARBLER
2. BLACKBURNIAN WARBLER, *a*. MALE; *b*. FEMALE
3. AMERICAN REDSTART, *a*. MALE; *b*. FEMALE
4. CANADA WARBLER, *a*. MALE; *b*. FEMALE
5. KIRTLAND'S WARBLER, *a*. MALE; *b*. FEMALE
6. MYRTLE WARBLER, *a*. MALE IN SPRING; *b*. FEMALE IN AUTUMN
7. MAGNOLIA WARBLER, *a*. MALE IN SPRING; *b*. FEMALE
8. BAY-BREASTED WARBLER, *a*. MALE IN SPRING; *b*. AUTUMN
9. CHESTNUT-SIDED WARBLER, *a*. MALE IN SPRING; *b*. IMMATURE IN AUTUMN
10. CAPE MAY WARBLER, *a*. MALE; *b*. FEMALE
11. BLACK-POLL WARBLER, *a*. MALE; *b*. FEMALE; *c*. AUTUMN
12. BLACK AND WHITE WARBLER, MALE
13. BLACK-THROATED GREEN WARBLER, *a*. MALE IN SPRING; *b*. FEMALE IN SPRING; *c*. AUTUMN
14. PINE WARBLER
15. WESTERN PALM WARBLER
16. YELLOW PALM WARBLER
17. PRAIRIE WARBLER, MALE
18. LOUISIANA WATER-THRUSH
19. NORTHERN WATER-THRUSH
20. OVEN-BIRD

presence of wing-bars and streaks along the sides, and the lack of yellow 'spectacles.'

PRAIRIE WARBLER. *Dendroica discolor discolor.*
This is the only Warbler with yellow under parts contrastingly streaked with black in which the stripings are *confined to the sides*. *Two* black face-marks, one through the eye and one below, are conclusive. At close range, in good light, some chestnut markings can be seen on the back; no other Warbler shares this feature. The sexes are similar.

FLORIDA PRAIRIE WARBLER. *Dendroica discolor collinsi.*
Peninsular Florida, chiefly along the coasts.

WESTERN PALM WARBLER. *Dendroica palmarum palmarum.*
Dull yellow, with a *chestnut-red* crown (duller in fall and winter); *constantly flicks its tail up and down.*
This tail-wagging habit will identify the species when no color or markings can be discerned. The Water-thrush *teeters*, in a quite different manner, more like a Spotted Sandpiper.

YELLOW PALM WARBLER. *Dendroica palmarum hypochrysea.*
Similar to the preceding, but much brighter yellow below; The Western Palm is dingier, *bright* yellow only on the under tail-coverts. In fall and winter the eye-stripe of the Western Palm Warbler is *whitish*, that of the Yellow Palm, yellow.

OVEN-BIRD. *Seiurus aurocapillus.*
A Sparrow-sized ground Warbler of the leafy woodlands; has somewhat the appearance of a Thrush — olive-brown above, but *striped*, rather than spotted, beneath. A *light orange stripe or patch* on the top of the head, visible at close range, is responsible for the rather appropriate old-fashioned name 'Golden-crowned Thrush.' It is usually seen *walking* on pale *pinkish* legs over the leaves or along some mossy log.
The song is an emphatic *teacher*, TEACHER, TEACHER, etc., repeated rapidly, louder and louder, till the air fairly rings with the vibrant accents.

NORTHERN WATER-THRUSH. *Seiurus noveboracensis noveboracensis.*

The Water-Thrushes are brown-backed birds about the size of a small Sparrow, with a *conspicuous light stripe over the eye*, and *heavily striped under parts*. Though Warblers by anatomical structure, their life in the flooded bottom lands and wooded swamps has made them ridiculously like little Sandpipers; when not running along some half-submerged log, they are constantly *teetering* up and down in much the manner of the 'spotties' of the shore.

The Northern Water-Thrush can be distinguished from the similar Louisiana by the *yellowness* of its under parts and, in good light, by the *yellowish* line over the eye. The under parts of the Louisiana may sometimes be slightly tinged with yellow, but the eye-stripe is always *pure white*.

A comparison of the songs of the two Water-Thrushes may be helpful. The songs of both are quite wild and musical; the thing to be remembered is that that of the Northern ends in a diagnostic *chew-chew-chew*.

GRINNELL'S WATER-THRUSH. *Seiurus noveboracensis notabilis*.

Not safely separable in the field from the other two Water-Thrushes, as the characters are not constant. It resembles both birds somewhat.

LOUISIANA WATER-THRUSH. *Seiurus motacilla*. See Northern Water-Thrush.

KENTUCKY WARBLER. *Oporornis formosus*.

A bird of the thickets; plain olive-green above, bright yellow below; partial yellow eye-ring or '*spectacles*,' and *black* '*sideburns*' or '*whiskers*' extending from the eye down the side of the yellow throat.

The Maryland Yellow-throat lacks the yellow 'spectacles' and is whitish on the belly; the Kentucky is solid yellow below. The Canada Warbler has similar spectacles, but is *gray* above, not olive, and usually shows some trace of the dark 'necklace' markings.

The song is a loud ringing *turtle, turtle, turtle*, very suggestive of the song of the Carolina Wren.

CONNECTICUT WARBLER. *Oporornis agilis*.

Two species of Warblers, both thicket-inhabiting birds,

possess a gray head and neck, or *hood*, contrasting with the yellow and olive of their body-plumage. The present species is at once recognized by the *round white eye-ring*. The other, the Mourning Warbler, lacks this. The Nashville Warbler is of a similar color-scheme, white eye-ring and all, but the throat is *yellow*, not gray.

Females and young are duller, with less gray, but there is always an obvious suggestion of a hood (usually like a brownish stain across the yellow of the under parts). The white eye-ring is always present. Another good point is the length of the yellow under tail-coverts, which reach nearly to the end of the tail. In the Mourning they reach but half way.

A common characteristic of the Connecticut Warbler is to flush from the low vegetation and to fly to some perch halfway up a nearby tree, where Thrush-like it watches its disturber with wide dreamy eyes.

MOURNING WARBLER. *Oporornis philadelphia.*

Olive above, yellow below, with a *gray hood* completely encircling the head and neck; *male* with an apron of *black crape* on the upper breast where the hood meets the yellow. Neither sex has the conspicuous white eye-ring of the Connecticut. The male Connecticut never has the black crape.

Females and immatures may occasionally have traces of an eye-ring, but never conspicuously. The length of the under tail-coverts is a good mark when it can be seen (see Connecticut Warbler).

The song of the male might be interpreted as *tiddle, tiddle, turtle, turtle,* the voice falling on the last two notes. There is considerable variation, but, as with all members of the genus *Oporornis,* the ringing, Carolina-Wren-like 'turtling' is evident.

MACGILLIVRAY'S WARBLER. *Oporornis tolmiei.*

Casual in migration in the Mississippi valley. Similar to the Connecticut and Mourning Warblers, the male possessing the distinctive features of both — the conspicuous *white eye-ring* of the Connecticut and the *black crape* of the Mourning. Females and immatures are not safely distinguishable.

NORTHERN YELLOW-THROAT. *Geothlypis trichas brachidac-tyla.*

The *male* with its *black mask*, or 'domino,' needs no detailed description.

Females and immature birds are plain olive-colored with a yellow throat and breast. The black mask is absent. They may be distinguished from any other similar Warblers by the *whitish* belly (the others are solid yellow below) and by the swampy habitat.

The song, one of the most easily recognized of bird-songs, is most commonly rendered *witchity-witchity-witchity-witch.*

MARYLAND YELLOW-THROAT. *Geothlypis trichas trichas.*

Breeds from southern Pennsylvania south, except in the territory occupied by the following race.

FLORIDA YELLOW-THROAT. *Geothlypis trichas ignota.*

Breeds from Florida north to central Alabama and Georgia, west along the Gulf to Louisiana, and north along the Atlantic coast to the Dismal Swamp in Virginia.

YELLOW-BREASTED CHAT. *Icteria virens virens.*

Except for its color, the Chat seems more like a Catbird or a Mocker than a Warbler. Its superior size (considerably larger than a Sparrow), its rather long tail, its eccentric song and actions, and its brushy habitat, all suggest those larger birds.

Both sexes are plain olive-green above, with white 'spectacles'; the throat and breast are bright yellow; the belly white. The long tail and the large size at once eliminate the possibility of it being any other Warbler. The Yellow-throated Vireo is colored similarly, but is smaller, with two white wing-bars.

HOODED WARBLER. *Wilsonia citrina.*

The black 'hood' of the *male* completely encircles the head and neck; this, and the yellow face and forehead, which stand out as a bright spot superimposed on the black, are determinative. The back is olive; the under parts yellow.

Females, both adult and young, are plain olive above and bright yellow on the *forehead* and under parts. Aside from a bit of white in the tail, the bird is *without streaks, wing-bars, or distinctive marks of any kind.* It is almost identical with the female Wilson's Warbler except for the larger size and *black* bill.

WILSON'S WARBLER. *Wilsonia pusilla pusilla.*
Male: — A yellow Warbler with a *round black cap.*
Females and immature birds may, or may not, show traces of the black cap. If they do not, they appear as small, plain Warblers, olive-green above and bright yellow below, with *no streaks, wing-bars, or marks of any kind.* The aspect of the round, beady black eye superimposed on the yellow face is an aid. The female Hooded shows white spots in the tail; the Yellow Warbler, yellow.

CANADA WARBLER. *Wilsonia canadensis.*
Plain gray above, bright yellow below; *male* with a *necklace of short black stripes* across the breast.
Females and immature birds are similar, but the necklace is fainter, sometimes nearly wanting. In any plumage the *gray* color of the upper parts in connection with the *total lack of white in the wings and tail* is conclusive.

AMERICAN REDSTART. *Setophaga ruticilla.*
The Redstart is one of the most butterfly-like of birds. As if consciously proud of its striking flash-pattern, it is constantly flitting about in sprightly fashion, drooping its wings and spreading fanwise its tail as if to make all who take notice admire.
Male: — Largely black with *bright orange patches on the wings and tail;* belly white. The only other small bird similarly colored is the Blackburnian Warbler, which, however, has the orange confined to the head, throat, and upper breast.
Female: — Chiefly olive-brown above, white below, with large *yellow* flash-patches on the wings and tail.
Immature male: — Considerable variation; much like the female; yellow often perceptibly tinged with orange.
The typical Redstart pattern is obvious in any plumage.

WEAVER FINCHES: PLOCEIDÆ

HOUSE, OR ENGLISH, SPARROW. *Passer domesticus domesticus.*
A species with which everybody is familiar.

EUROPEAN TREE SPARROW. *Passer montanus montanus.*
An introduced species, resident about St. Louis, Missouri.
Both sexes resemble the male House Sparrow, with the black
throat-patch, but are distinctively marked with a *large black
spot* behind the eye.

MEADOWLARKS, BLACKBIRDS, AND ORIOLES: ICTERIDÆ

As members of this group are so vastly different, it is difficult to make any generalizations for use in the field, except
that they have conical, sharp-pointed bills and rather flat profiles. They are best characterized under their various species.

BOBOLINK. *Dolichonyx oryzivorus.*
Male in spring: — The only song-bird that is *black below
and largely white above*, a direct reversal of the normal tone-
pattern of other birds, which are almost invariably lighter
below.
Female and autumn birds: — These are the 'Reedbirds' of
the Southern marshes; somewhat larger than Sparrows,
largely yellowish-buff with dark stripings on the crown and
upper parts. The yellowish color and the note, a metallic
pink, are distinctive.

EASTERN MEADOWLARK. *Sturnella magna magna.*
Our first acquaintance with the Meadowlark usually comes
early in our studies. On crossing some extensive field or
meadow, a rather large, chunky brown bird flushes from the
grass, showing a conspicuous patch of *white* on each side of
the short, wide tail. The only other ground-dwelling birds
that show similar white outer tail-feathers are the Pipit,
Vesper Sparrow, and Junco, all of which are very much
smaller, with the slimmer proportions of Sparrows. Should
we see a Meadowlark perched on some distant fencepost, our
glass will reveal a bright yellow breast crossed by a black V,
or gorget.
The Flicker is similarly sized and brown above, but with
a white *rump* instead of white sides of the tail, and it flies in
a very different, *bounding* manner. The Starling is perhaps

the closest to the Meadowlark in general build. When both birds are silhouetted, or too distant for color to register, the Meadowlark can be picked out by its different flight — several short, rapid wing-beats alternated with short periods of sailing.

SOUTHERN MEADOWLARK. *Sturnella magna argutula.*
A smaller, darker race of the Meadowlark, with a huskier, wheezier song, breeding from South Carolina and southern Illinois south to Florida and Louisiana.

WESTERN MEADOWLARK. *Sturnella neglecta.*
Casual east to Illinois and Michigan. Nearly identical with the Eastern Meadowlark, but paler; best recognized in the field by its song, providing the observer is acquainted with the variations of that of the Eastern bird. The Eastern Meadowlark has a clear-cut whistled call of several syllables; the corresponding vocal performance of the Western species is a mellow, bubbling affair.

YELLOW-HEADED BLACKBIRD. *Xanthocephalus xanthocephalus.*
A Robin-sized Blackbird with a *yellow* head — totally unlike anything else; shows a conspicuous white patch in the wing in flight. Females are similar to the males but are smaller and duller with most of the yellow confined to the throat.

EASTERN RED-WING. *Agelaius phœniceus phœniceus.*
Male: — Black, with *red epaulets* at the bend of the wings. Absolutely unmistakable. Often, when at rest, the scarlet is concealed, only the buffy or yellowish margin of the red patch being visible.
Immature male: — Dusky-brown, but with the scarlet patches of the adult male.
Female and young: — Brownish; identified by the sharp-pointed bill, Blackbird appearance, and *well-defined stripings* below. Bobolinks often frequent marshes in the fall but are yellowish, without the heavily streaked under parts.
Several subspecies besides the Eastern Red-wing are recognized. Two interior forms, the GIANT RED-WING (*A. p. arctolegus*) and the THICK-BILLED RED-WING (*A. p. fortis*)

occasionally straggle eastward in migration. Neither is distinguishable in life. The three Southern forms can be identified by the locality in which they are found breeding.

FLORIDA RED-WING. *Agelaius phœniceus mearnsi.*

Resident from the Okeefinokee Swamp in Georgia south through most of Florida except those portions occupied by the two following races. The Eastern Red-wing apparently works down to the extreme north-central portion of Florida as a breeder.

Females of this and the following subspecies are very much duskier than the female Eastern Red-wing.

MAYNARD'S RED-WING. *Agelaius phœniceus floridanus.*

Southern Florida, south of Lake Okeechobee.

GULF COAST RED-WING. *Agelaius phœniceus littoralis.*

Breeds along the Gulf Coast from Choctawatchee Bay, Florida, west.

ORCHARD ORIOLE. *Icterus spurius.*

Smaller than a Robin.

Adult male: — *Chestnut and black;* head, neck, back, wings, and tail black; rump and belly deep chestnut. The Baltimore Oriole is fiery orange and black.

Immature male: — Greenish above, yellow below, with a *black throat.* Some female Baltimore Orioles have black throats, but such birds will appear more orange than green.

Females and young: — Olive above, yellow below, with two white wing-bars; difficult to distinguish from females and young of the Baltimore Oriole, but decidedly *greener.*

BALTIMORE ORIOLE. *Icterus galbula.*

Smaller than a Robin.

Male: — *Fiery orange and black.* The male Redstart and the Blackburnian Warbler, the only other species colored with such intense orange, are both considerably smaller than Sparrows.

Female and young: — Olive above, yellow below, with two wing-bars; very similar to the female Orchard Oriole, but decidedly more orange-yellow. Female Orioles resemble female Tanagers in general coloration, but the latter birds show no wing-bars (except the accidental Western Tanager).

Bullock's Oriole. *Icterus bullocki.*
Accidental in the East. The *male* is fiery orange and black, much like the male Baltimore Oriole, but has *orange cheeks* and an *orange line over the eye* (the head of the Baltimore Oriole is solid black).

Rusty Blackbird. *Euphagus carolinus.*
Male in spring: — A Robin-sized Blackbird with a whitish eye; frequents wet places, woodland swamps, etc.
Female in spring: — Slate-colored.
Adults and young in autumn and winter: — More or less tinged with rusty; closely *barred* beneath.
Grackles are the long-tailed Blackbirds, Starlings the short; the Red-wing, Cowbird, and Rusty are all of more equal proportions. The Grackles are the only other Blackbirds with whitish eyes, but the larger size, ample *rounded* or *keel-shaped* tail, and, in strong light, the bright metallic reflections, will identify them. Male Red-wings have red epaulets; females, heavy black *stripings* beneath. Cowbirds are smaller, *dark-eyed* and *thick-billed.*
The 'song' of the Rusty Blackbird sounds like the creaking of a rusty hinge, rather penetrating but not altogether unmelodious.

Brewer's Blackbird. *Euphagus cyanocephalus.*
Casual in migration in the Southern States; similar to the Rusty Blackbird, but *male* with *purplish*, instead of greenish, head reflections, and *female* with *dark brown*, instead of yellowish, eyes; in no plumage is the bird washed with rusty or ochre.

Boat-tailed Grackle. *Cassidix mexicanus.*
The Boat-tail, or 'Jackdaw,' is at once recognized by its large size; the Florida Purple Grackle is but one or two inches larger than a Robin; the Boat-tail, very much larger. *Females* are brown, not black, and are *much* smaller than the males; in the other Grackles there is no such great difference between the sexes.
As a species, the Boat-tailed Grackle is chiefly maritime, occurring along the South Atlantic and Gulf coasts south of

the Chesapeake, but in Florida the bird apparently finds conditions to its liking throughout the peninsula.

PURPLE GRACKLE. *Quiscalus quiscula quiscula.*

Grackles are the familiar large blackbirds, larger than Robins, with the long, wedge-shaped tails. A crease in the center often gives the tail a keel-shaped appearance when the bird is in the air. The line of flight is more even, not as undulating as that of other Blackbirds.

The present subspecies is the breeding Grackle of the Middle Atlantic Coast region from southern New England and the lower Hudson Valley south.

BRONZED GRACKLE. *Quiscalus quiscula æneus.*

The 'Crow Blackbird' of the greater part of the eastern United States. In strong light the back reflects a *bright even bronze* color; that of the Purple, purple and bronze, broken by *short iridescent bars.*

FLORIDA GRACKLE. *Quiscalus quiscula aglæus.*

Breeds along the Atlantic Coast from South Carolina to Florida, and westward along the Gulf. Similar to the Purple Grackle, but in strong light the back reflects a bright *bottle-green.*

COWBIRD. *Molothrus ater ater.*

A rather small Blackbird (about eight inches) with a short, conical, Sparrow-like bill.

The *male* is the only black bird with a *brown* head. The *female* is uniformly gray. The only other entirely gray birds are the Catbird, which is slimmer, with *chestnut* under tail-coverts, and the young Starling, which is chunkier, shorter-tailed, and longer-billed.

When mixed in with other Blackbirds, Cowbirds are obviously smaller and walk about with their tails lifted high off the ground. The song is a liquid *gluck-glee.*

TANAGERS: THRAUPIDÆ

The males of the group are among the most brilliant-colored of birds, the three species occurring in the East possessing more or less bright red. Females are duller, green above and yellow below, a little like large Warblers or Vireos; they are somewhat larger than House Sparrows. The Tanagers are most likely to be confused with Orioles, but are sluggish, much less active.

WESTERN TANAGER. *Piranga ludoviciana.*
Accidental in the East.
Male: — Yellow and black, with a *red face.* Totally unlike any other American bird. Males in autumn lose most of the red.
Female: — Similar to the other Tanagers, dull greenish above, and yellowish below. Both sexes possess broad *yellow wing-bars,* which are absent in the two Eastern species.

SCARLET TANAGER. *Piranga erythromelas.*
Male: — The only bright red bird with *black* wings and tail. The Summer Tanager and the Cardinal are more extensively red, wings and tail included.
Female, immature, and winter male: — Dull green above and yellowish below, with dusky or blackish wings. Their sluggish actions and large size (larger than House Sparrow) distinguish them from the Warblers and Vireos; the lack of wing-bars and greener coloration, from female Orioles.
Changing male: — Males changing from summer to winter plumage, or *vice versa,* are more or less patched with scarlet, yellowish, and green. Should such a bird arouse hopes of a Western Tanager, it should be remembered that that bird is black-backed with broad yellow wing-bars.

SUMMER TANAGER. *Piranga rubra rubra.*
Male: — Bright rose-red *all over* (Scarlet Tanager has black wings and tail; Cardinal, a crest).
Female: — Olive above, deep yellow below. The wings are not dusky or blackish as in the female Scarlet Tanager, and the under parts are more orange. The bird is of much the color of a female Oriole but lacks the wing-bars.
Immature males acquiring the adult plumage may be patched with red and green, but do not possess the black wings of the similarly plumaged Scarlet Tanager.

GROSBEAKS, FINCHES, SPARROWS, AND BUNTINGS: FRINGILLIDÆ

The best character by which this family can be recognized is the bill, which is short and stout, adapted for seed-cracking. The two birds not belonging to this group which are most apt to be mistaken for *Fringillidæ*, because of their stout, conical bills, are the Cowbird and the Bobolink.

Three types of bills exist within the group: that of the Grosbeak, extremely large, thick, and rounded in outline; the more ordinary Canary-like bill, possessed by most of the Finches, Sparrows, and Buntings; and that of the Crossbill, the mandibles of which are crossed, somewhat like pruning shears, at the tips.

Many of the Grosbeaks, Finches, and Buntings are highly colored, in contrast to the Sparrows, which are, for the most part, plain, streaked with brown.

EASTERN CARDINAL. *Richmondena cardinalis cardinalis.*
Male: — Smaller than a Robin; all red except for a black patch about the bill; *the only red bird with a crest.*
Female: — Largely yellowish-brown, with some red; at once recognizable by the crest and heavy red bill.
FLORIDA CARDINAL. *Richmondena cardinalis floridanus.* Peninsular Florida.
LOUISIANA CARDINAL. *Richmondena cardinalis magnirostris.* Southern Louisiana.

ROSE-BREASTED GROSBEAK. *Hedymeles ludovicianus.*
Male: — Black and white, with a large triangular patch of *rose-red* on the breast. In flight a ring of white flashes across the black of the upper plumage.
Female: — Very different; streaked, like a large, overgrown Sparrow; may be recognized by the large Grosbeak bill, broad white wing-bars, and a conspicuous white line over the eye; resembles considerably in pattern a female Purple Finch.

EASTERN BLUE GROSBEAK. *Guiraca cærulea cærulea.*
Male: — Deep dull blue; appears black at a distance, the bird then resembling a Cowbird. The only other *all-blue* bird

GROSBEAKS, FINCHES, BUNTINGS, ETC.

1. PINE GROSBEAK, *a.* ADULT MALE; *b.* IMMATURE MALE; *c.* FEMALE

2. CARDINAL, *a.* MALE; *b.* FEMALE

3. PURPLE FINCH, *a.* MALE; *b.* FEMALE

4. WHITE-WINGED CROSSBILL, *a.* MALE; *b.* FEMALE

5. RED CROSSBILL, *a.* MALE; *b.* FEMALE

6. GOLDFINCH, *a.* MALE; *b.* FEMALE

7. PINE SISKIN

8. COMMON REDPOLL, *a.* MALE; *b.* FEMALE

9. BLUE GROSBEAK, *a.* MALE; *b.* FEMALE

10. EVENING GROSBEAK, *a.* MALE; *b.* FEMALE

11. INDIGO BUNTING, *a.* MALE; *b.* FEMALE

12. ROSE-BREASTED GROSBEAK, *a.* MALE IN SPRING; *b.* FEMALE

13. PAINTED BUNTING, *a.* MALE; *b.* FEMALE

14. RED-EYED TOWHEE, *a.* MALE; *b.* FEMALE

15. DICKCISSEL, MALE

16. SLATE-COLORED JUNCO, MALE IN SPRING

17. SNOW BUNTING, *a.* MALE IN WINTER; *b.* FEMALE

18. SMITH'S LONGSPUR, *a.* MALE IN WINTER; *b.* MALE IN SPRING

19. LAPLAND LONGSPUR, *a.* MALE IN WINTER; *b.* MALE IN SPRING

is the Indigo Bunting. The Grosbeak is larger than the Bunting, with a much larger bill, and shows two *chestnut-brown* wing-bars. (See immature male Indigo Bunting.)

Female: — Larger than a House Sparrow, or about the size of a Cowbird; brown, lighter below, with two *buffy* wing-bars. The female Indigo Bunting is smaller, without the wing-bars and the Grosbeak bill.

INDIGO BUNTING. *Passerina cyanea.*

Male: — Smaller than a House Sparrow; deep, rich blue *all over*. In autumn the male becomes more like the brown female, but there is always enough blue in the wings and tail to identify it.

Female: — Plain brown, paler on the under parts; *the only small brown Finch that is devoid of obvious stripings, wing-bars, or other distinctive marks.*

Immature male: — Brown and blue; some individuals may resemble Blue Grosbeaks but are much smaller (slightly larger than a Chipping Sparrow), with a smaller, more Sparrow-like bill.

PAINTED BUNTING. *Passerina ciris.*

Of all our birds this is undoubtedly the most gaudily colored. The male is a little chippy-sized Finch, a patchwork of *bright red, green, and indigo* — blue-violet on the head, green on the back, red on the rump and under parts.

The female is very plain — greenish above, paling to lemon-green below; *no other small Finch is green.*

DICKCISSEL. *Spiza americana.*

About the size and build of a House Sparrow; *male,* suggestive of a tiny Meadowlark, with a yellow breast and black bib; *female,* very much like a female House Sparrow, but paler, with a much whiter stripe over the eye, and a touch of yellow on the breast. The chestnut bend of the wing is also distinctive.

The Dickcissel is a frequenter of open country, with an especial fondness for alfalfa fields. In such places its song might be heard, a staccato, mechanical-sounding rendering of its name — *dick-dick-dick-cissel.*

EASTERN EVENING GROSBEAK. *Hesperiphona vespertina vespertina.*

A large, chunky, short-tailed Finch, nearly the size of a Starling. The yellowish color, and the extremely large, conical, whitish bill distinguish it at once from anything else. A-wing, it is recognized as a Finch by the characteristic undulating flight and is distinguished from the Pine Grosbeak, the only winter Finch of similar size, by the shorter tail. The large white wing-patches show at a great distance in flight. The Snow Bunting is the only other northern Finch showing so much white in the wing.

The *male* is largely yellow, with black and white wings, suggesting an overgrown Goldfinch. *Females* are gray, but with just enough of the yellow and the black and white to be recognizable. The female Pine Grosbeak is slimmer, with a smaller, *dark* bill, much less white in the wing, *none in the tail.*

The note sounds like a ringing, glorified chirp of a House Sparrow.

EASTERN PURPLE FINCH. *Carpodacus purpureus purpureus.*

Purple is hardly the word; raspberry or old-rose is more like it. The *male* is about the size of a House Sparrow, rosy-red, brightest on the head and rump. The Pine Grosbeak is similarly colored but is much larger, nearer the size of a Robin. Redpolls are red only on the forehead, not on the entire head.

The *female* is a heavily striped brown Sparrow-like bird with a broad, whitish line over the eye. The large, stout bill distinguishes it from the streaked Sparrows.

Immature males resemble females.

The note, a dull metallic *tick*, is useful, once learned.

PINE GROSBEAK. *Pinicola enucleator leucura.*

The largest of the northern Finches; near the size of a Robin.

Male: — The large size, the rosy-red color, and the two white wing-bars identify it. (The White-winged Crossbill is rosy-red with white wing-bars, but is smaller, with a slender, cross-tipped bill.)

Female: — Gray with two white wing-bars; head and rump tinged with yellow.

Immature male: — Similar to the female but with a touch of red on the head and rump.

A Robin-sized winter Finch is quite surely this species. The Evening Grosbeak is shorter with more Starling-like proportions.

All Finches rise and fall in their flight, but this one is a regular 'roller-coaster.' Each drop may be accompanied by a clear, three-syllabled whistle, *tee-tee-tew,* a call that sounds remarkably like the whistled cry of the Greater Yellow-legs.

NEWFOUNDLAND PINE GROSBEAK. *Pinicola enucleator eschatosus.*

A smaller race, resident in Newfoundland. It wanders south to New England in winter, but it is probably not recognizable in life.

BRITISH GOLDFINCH. *Carduelis carduelis britannica.*

Slightly larger than the common Goldfinch; cinnamon-brown with a *bright red* patch about the base of the bill and a *broad yellow band* crossing the wing. The sexes are similar. Introduced.

HOARY REDPOLL. *Acanthus hornemanni exilipes.*

Very similar to the Common Redpoll, but smaller and whiter. The white rump, *devoid of streakings,* is the best mark.

COMMON REDPOLL. *Acanthus linaria linaria.*

In notes, size, shape, and actions Redpolls resemble Goldfinches and Siskins; little streaked, gray-brown birds that may be known in any plumage by a *bright red cap* on the forehead and a *black chin. Males* are pink-breasted.

Purple Finches are larger and redder (the *entire head* and much of the back and under parts are reddish); Siskins are darker with more heavily-striped under parts.

GREATER REDPOLL. *Acanthus linaria rostrata.*

Somewhat larger, darker- and larger-billed than the Common Redpoll. This difference is fairly obvious when the two birds are together in the same flock.

PINE SISKIN. *Spinus pinus pinus.*

A small, *heavily streaked* brown Finch with a *flash of yellow* in the wing and tail. In size and actions it much resembles the Goldfinch; the song and notes, though similar, are more coarse and wheezy.

Winter Goldfinches are unstreaked; Redpolls are paler, without the heavy streakings across the front of the breast; the female Purple Finch is similar, but larger (size of a House Sparrow) with a larger bill. None of these three shows any yellow in either wings or tail.

The commonest calls are a simple *tit-i-tit* and a long buzzy *shreeeee* — the latter quite unique among bird-notes.

EASTERN GOLDFINCH. *Spinus tristis tristis.*

Smaller than a House Sparrow.

Male in summer: — *The only small yellow bird with black wings.* The Yellow Warbler, which shares with this bird the nicknames 'Yellow-bird' and 'Wild Canary,' is yellow all over.

Female in summer: — Dull olive yellow with blackish wings; distinguished from any other small olive-yellow bird (Warblers, etc.) by its stout Finch bill.

Winter birds: — Much like the summer female. The only two similar small winter Finches, the Redpoll and the Siskin, are *streaked;* the Goldfinch is evenly colored above and below.

The flight is extremely undulating; often the dips are punctuated by a simple *ti-teé-di-di.*

RED CROSSBILL. *Loxia curvirostra pusilla.*

Size near that of a House Sparrow; feeds mainly on the cones of evergreen trees, the cracking of which often betrays their presence. The crossed, pruning-shear mandibles are distinctive; at a distance, when the crossed tips are not visible, the comparative slenderness of the bill is obvious (the bills of other Finches are relatively shorter and stouter).

Male: — *Brick red,* brighter on the rump; wings and tail dark. Several of the other northern Finches are *rosy-red,* but this is the only brick-red bird of the group.

Female and young: — Dull olive-gray; yellowish on the rump and under parts. The plain dark wings distinguish this species from the White-winged Crossbill.

NEWFOUNDLAND CROSSBILL. *Loxia curvirostra percna.*

It is perfectly possible to identify typical individuals of this subspecies of the Red Crossbill in the field, especially if one is well acquainted with the commoner bird. It is larger, especially the bill; the comparison is a little like that of the bills of the Downy and Hairy Woodpeckers. Males are darker, with the red rump more glowing in color; females are also darker, hence the yellow rump shows to better advantage. The notes are louder; in brief, it is a Red Crossbill intensified. Extremes are at once recognizable, but, as with most subspecies, many specimens can be properly determined only by collecting.

During those rare occasions when it enters the United States, on account of a shortage in the cone-crop to the north, it is most likely (though not always) to be found at various coastal points where pitch pines are numerous.

WHITE-WINGED CROSSBILL. *Loxia leucoptera.*

Male: — Size of a House Sparrow; *rosy-pink* with black wings and tail and *two broad white wing-bars*. The Pine Grosbeak is rosy, with white wing-bars, but is much larger (near the size of a Robin).

Female and young: — Olive-gray with a yellowish rump, like the Red Crossbill, but with *two broad white wing-bars*.

The wing-bars are often quite evident when the birds are in flight and help in picking out individuals of this species from mixed flocks of Crossbills.

A comparison of the notes of the two Crossbills will help. The common notes of the White-wing are a sweet *peet* and a dry *chif-chif.* The note corresponding to the *chif-chif* in the Red Crossbill is a hard *pip* or *pip-pip.*

RED-EYED TOWHEE; CHEWINK. *Pipilo erythrophthalmus erythrophthalmus.*

Smaller and more slender than a Robin, which it slightly resembles; the reddish is confined to the sides. It frequents brushy places, where its presence can often be detected by its noisy rummaging among the dead leaves. The call is a loud, easily recognized *chewink!*

Male: — Entire head and upper parts black; *sides Robin-*

red; belly white. In flight the bird looks black, with much white showing toward the tips of its long, ample tail.

Female and young: — Similar, but brown where the male is black.

ALABAMA TOWHEE. *Pipilo erythrophthalmus canaster.*

This subspecies inhabits Alabama, central Georgia, and part of northern Florida, west of the peninsula. It is apparently the connecting link between the preceding red-eyed form and the White-eyed Towhee.

WHITE-EYED TOWHEE. *Pipilo erythrophthalmus alleni.*

The breeding Towhee of the South Atlantic coast from South Carolina to and including the whole Florida Peninsula; resembles the Red-eyed Towhee, but the iris is *white*. The call, corresponding to the clearly-enunciated *chewink* of the other bird, is a higher-pitched, wheezy *zree.*

ARCTIC TOWHEE. *Pipilo maculatus arcticus.*

Casual east to Illinois. Similar to the eastern Towhee, but has more white in the wing, and *several rows of white spots* on the back and scapulars.

LARK BUNTING. *Calamospiza melanocorys.*

Accidental in the East. The *male in spring* looks like a small Blackbird (about House Sparrow size) with *large white wing-patches.* (Bobolink has much white *on the back* as well as on the wings; both are open-country birds.)

Females, young, and *autumn males* are brown with stripings on the breast; they slightly resemble female Purple Finches except for the whitish wing-patches.

IPSWICH SPARROW. *Passerculus princeps.*

A large pale *sandy-colored* Sparrow; in spring it has a pale yellow line over the eye; frequents the coarse growths of beach grass among the dunes along the ocean.

In pattern it resembles a Savannah Sparrow, but it is so much larger and paler that it would not be confused with it. It is more like a Vesper Sparrow, but has a white stripe through the center of the crown and lacks the white outer tail-feathers.

EASTERN SAVANNAH SPARROW. *Passerculus sandwichensis savanna.*

FOX

VESPER — WHITE OUTER TAIL FEATHERS

REDDISH TAIL

LINCOLN'S — BUFFY BREAST BAND

SONG — LARGE CENTRAL BREAST SPOT

IPSWICH — PALE COLORATION

SAVANNAH — YELLOWISH EYE-STRIPE

SEASIDE — SHORT YELLOW EYE-LINE

SHARP-TAILED — OCHRE-BUFF FACE, OCHRE-BUFF UNDERPARTS

LECONTE'S — REDDISH COLLAR

GRASSHOPPER — UNSTREAKED UNDERPARTS

HENSLOW'S — OLIVE-COLORED HEAD

SPARROWS   I

Like a *short-tailed* Song Sparrow with a *yellowish stripe* over the eye *and pale pink legs*. The tail of a Savannah Sparrow is slightly forked, not rounded like that of the Song Sparrow. This obvious fork is an aid to the observer flushing Sparrows from the salt meadow where both Savannahs and Sharp-tails are common.

The song is a dreamy, lisping, *tsit-tsit-tsit-tseeeee-tseeee.* At a distance the three opening notes are inaudible.

LABRADOR SAVANNAH SPARROW. *Passerculus sandwichensis labradorius.*

Breeds in Labrador. Darker and more heavily streaked on the breast than the Eastern Savannah Sparrow.

EASTERN GRASSHOPPER SPARROW. *Ammodramus savannarum australis.*

A short-tailed, flat-headed little Sparrow; differs from the other Sparrows of the open fields in having an *unstreaked* dingy breast.

Young birds with streaked breasts complicate matters. They then resemble the adult Henslow's Sparrow, but are not so reddish on the wings as that bird.

The song is a lengthy bubbling insect-like buzz.

FLORIDA GRASSHOPPER SPARROW. *Ammodramus savannarum floridanus.*

Breeds in the prairie regions of central Florida; upper parts mainly *black* instead of reddish.

LECONTE'S SPARROW. *Passerherbulus caudacutus.*

A sharp-tailed Sparrow of the marshes, characterized by the *bright buffy-ochre* of the eye-line, throat, and breast, and the wide *pinkish-brown collar* on the nape of the adult.

The ochre of the under parts distinguishes it from both the Henslow's and the Grasshopper Sparrow; the buffier *throat* and the *white stripe* through the center of the crown, from the three Sharp-tails.

EASTERN HENSLOW'S SPARROW. *Passerherbulus henslowi susurrans.*

Short-tailed and big-headed; finely streaked below with black. The striped *olive-colored* head in conjunction with the *reddish*; wings will identify it. The only other Sharp-tailed

Sparrow of the open meadow (not salt marsh) is the Grass-hopper Sparrow, which is clear-breasted.

The Henslow's is most commonly seen perched atop a weed, from which it gives utterance to one of the poorest vocal efforts of any bird; throwing back its head, it ejects a hiccoughing *tsi-lick*. As if to practice this 'song,' so that it might not always remain at the bottom of the list, it frequently hiccoughs all night long. In places where both this bird and the Short-billed Marsh Wren occur together, the two hold moonlight concerts, if we may call them such.

In late summer young Grasshopper Sparrows are streaked and resemble adult Henslow's; young Henslow's are practically without breast-streakings, thus resembling the adult Grass-hopper Sparrow. Something surely went amiss here. The Henslow's Sparrow, however, always has more or less russet on the wing.

SHARP-TAILED SPARROW. *Ammospiza caudacuta caudacuta.*

Sharp-tailed Sparrows are identified by the *ochre-yellow areas of the face*, which completely surround the gray of the ear-patch. The present subspecies, the breeding Sharp-tail of the salt marsh from Massachusetts to Virginia, may be told from the others by the *sharply defined dark breast-streakings*. Even in young birds, which are often so buffy below that they resemble Nelson's Sparrows, this point holds.

The Savannah Sparrow, another frequenter of the salt marsh, has a *forked* tail. This is evident when the bird flushes from the grass and flies away from the observer.

NELSON'S SPARROW. *Ammospiza caudacuta nelsoni.*

Inland, about fresh-water marshes, in the fall migration the Nelson's Sparrow is the Sharp-tail that is most apt to occur, although the Acadian may be found rarely in some localities. The Common Sharp-tail, being more strictly coastal, never is.

The Nelson's is best distinguished by its bright ochre-buff breast, which is *almost devoid of streakings*. In short, the Nel-son's has very little noticeable breast-streaking; the Acadian has pale, blurry streaks; and the Common Sharp-tail has sharply-defined breast-marks.

The present bird has a contrastingly marked back like the

Common Sharp-tail, while that of the Acadian is faded out. This will help in inland localities where the Common Sharp-tail need not be considered.

Squeaking will often induce these shy Sparrows to show themselves in the open, where they can be more easily studied.

ACADIAN SHARP-TAILED SPARROW. *Ammospiza caudacuta subvirgata.*

In the autumn when all three Sharp-tails are gathered together in the same coastal marshes, every now and then a decidedly pale individual will flush from the grass. In the early days Audubon noticed this, but failed to recognize these birds as a different species. This grayer, more northern form is known as the Acadian Sharp-tail. Some individuals appear almost bluish as they fly up. Besides being paler and more washed out on the back, this subspecies is less buffy, the line over the eye is of a more lemon-yellow tinge, and the streakings on the breast are pale and *blurry*.

NORTHERN SEASIDE SPARROW. *Ammospiza maritima maritima.*

A dark, olive-gray, sharp-tailed Sparrow of the salt marsh; a short yellow line *before the eye* and a white streak along the jaw are characteristic. In general appearance it is dingier than any of the three Sharp-tails, without the conspicuous ochre head-markings.

The Seaside Sparrow has been split into more Eastern races than any other bird. The present form is the only one that occurs between Massachusetts and Virginia. The others may be recognized by the region in which they are found breeding. In parts of Florida, where several may winter in the same locality, it is folly to attempt discrimination without collecting. The breeding-ranges are given below.

MACGILLIVRAY'S SEASIDE SPARROW. *Ammospiza maritima macgillivraii.* Salt marshes from North Carolina to the South Edisto River, South Carolina.

WAYNE'S SEASIDE SPARROW. *Ammospiza maritima waynei.* Coast of Georgia.

SMYRNA SEASIDE SPARROW. *Ammospiza maritima pelonota.* Atlantic coast of northern Florida from Amelia Island to New Smyrna.

SCOTT'S SEASIDE SPARROW. *Ammospiza maritima peninsulæ.*
Gulf coast of Florida from Indian Pass to Pepperfish Keys.

WALKULLA SEASIDE SPARROW. *Ammospiza maritima juncicola.* Gulf coast of western Florida from St. Andrew's Bay westward.

HOWELL'S SEASIDE SPARROW. *Ammospiza maritima howelli.*
Gulf coast of Alabama and Mississippi.

LOUISIANA SEASIDE SPARROW. *Ammospiza maritima fisheri.*
Gulf Coast of Louisiana.

DUSKY SEASIDE SPARROW. *Ammospiza nigrescens.*
Resident of the salt marshes around Merritt Island, Florida. About the size of the Northern Seaside Sparrow, but *upper parts blackish,* and under parts heavily streaked with black. (The local name is 'Black Shore Finch.')

CAPE SABLE SEASIDE SPARROW. *Ammospiza mirabilis.*
Resident of the coastal prairie near Cape Sable in the southern tip of Florida; *no other Seaside Sparrow breeds in southern Florida;* greener above and whiter below than any race of *maritima.*

EASTERN VESPER SPARROW. *Poœcetes gramineus gramineus.*
The *white outer tail-feathers* flashing conspicuously as the bird flies make the best mark. Perched, the bird looks like a buffy Song Sparrow, without the large central breast-spot. A *chestnut-colored patch* at the bend of the wing is determinative.

Three other common open-country birds have white outer tail-feathers: the Meadowlark, which is very much larger and chunkier; the Junco, which is slate-gray, not brown; and the Pipit. The last-named bird is the most similar, but close scrutiny reveals that it is thin-billed, *walks* instead of hops, and constantly *wags its tail.*

EASTERN LARK SPARROW. *Chondestes grammacus grammacus.*
A handsomely marked open-country Sparrow with *chestnut* ear-patches, a white breast with one dark central spot, and *much white in the tail* (somewhat as in a Towhee — not as in a Vesper Sparrow).

BLACK AND WHITE CROWNS

GRAY THROAT

WHITE THROAT

WHITE-CROWNED

WHITE-THROATED

BROWN AND BUFF HEAD STRIPES

BLACK CROWN AND THROAT

WHITE-CROWNED
IMMATURE

CHESTNUT CHEEK-PATCH

HARRIS'S

LARK

WHITE TIPS

STRIPED CROWN
BROWN CHEEK PATCH

CENTRAL BREAST SPOT

CLAY-COLORED

WHITE THROAT

TREE

FOUR SPECIES
HAVE
RUFOUS-RED CAPS

SWAMP
ROUNDED TAIL

WHITE EYE-STRIPE
PINK BILL

CHIPPING

FIELD

SPARROWS II

Young birds are finely streaked on the breast and lack the central spot, but are otherwise quite recognizable.

PINE-WOODS SPARROW. *Aimophila æstivalis æstivalis.* In the piny woods of the South where a growth of scrub palmetto persists this shy little Sparrow may be found. It flushes rather reluctantly, and quickly drops back into the undergrowth, where it plays hide-and-seek with the observer. An occasional glimpse will show it to be a brown-backed bird with a *clear dingy-buff breast.* No other Sparrow is quite so plain in appearance.

The song is a melodious thrush-like performance.

BACHMAN'S SPARROW. *Aimophila æstivalis bachmani.*

This subspecies, the *grayer* of the two, enjoys the wider range, from Virginia and southern Ohio south. The Pine-woods Sparrow, the *browner* race, is the breeding bird of Florida and southeastern Georgia.

WHITE-WINGED JUNCO. *Junco aikeni.*

Like a Slate-colored Junco, but larger and paler with two white wing-bars and a slightly greater amount of white in the tail. All supposed specimens of the White-winged Junco taken in the East have proved to be aberrant individuals of the Slate-colored Junco.

SLATE-COLORED JUNCO. *Junco hyemalis hyemalis.*

Smaller than a House Sparrow; dark slate-gray with *conspicuous white outer tail-feathers;* belly white.

The Vesper Sparrow also shows a V of white formed by the white outer tail-feathers, but that bird is buffy-brown, not blackish. Streaked youngsters may be told from Vesper Sparrows by their duskier color and by the woodland habitat in which they are raised.

CAROLINA JUNCO. *Junco hyemalis carolinensis.*

The breeding Junco of the southern Alleghenies from Maryland to Georgia; very similar to the preceding.

OREGON JUNCO (*including subspecies*). *Junco oreganus.*

Accidental in the East; resembles the Slate-colored Junco, but back *russet-brown,* contrasting sharply with the black head; sides pinkish-brown.

Immature Slate-colored Juncos are sometimes pinkish on the sides but would not show the well-marked brown back. Young birds of this sort are sometimes misidentified as Pink-sided Juncos (*Junco mearnsi*), a bird that has never been taken in the East; *mearnsi* would be of a more evenly pale-gray color on the head and breast, without the evident brownish wash present in immature birds.

TREE SPARROW. *Spizella arborea arborea.*
A single *round black spot* in the center of the breast identifies the Tree Sparrow, or 'Winter Chippy.' A bright *red-brown cap* and two conspicuous white wing-bars are also character-istic.

CHIPPING SPARROW. *Spizella passerina passerina.*
A very small clear-breasted Sparrow with a bright *rufous cap* and a *black line* through the eye.
Young birds in late summer are finely streaked below but are recognized by their small size and moderately long forked tail. The juvenile Field Sparrow is similar, without the distinct striping on the crown. Young birds in autumn are more like the adults.

CLAY-COLORED SPARROW. *Spizella pallida.*
Casual in the East; a small open-country Sparrow, clear-breasted like the Field Sparrow and the Chippy, but with a *light stripe* through the center of the crown and a sharply out-lined *brown ear-patch.*
Fall immatures are even more like Chippies of the same age, but the crown is more distinctly striped and without much hint of rufous.

FIELD SPARROW. *Spizella pusilla pusilla.*
The reddish upper parts, clear breast, and *pink bill* are the Field Sparrow's obvious characters. Otherwise, it resembles the Tree Sparrow and the Chippy, except for the less notice-able facial striping; this and the eye-ring gives the bird a rather blank expression. Pasture Sparrow would be a better name than the one it carries, as it does not live in open fields.
Young birds in the *juvenile plumage* (summer) are finely

streaked below like young Chippies in the same plumage,but do not have the well-marked head-stripings.

HARRIS'S SPARROW. *Zonotrichia querula.*

Very large, larger than a House Sparrow, or near the size of a Fox Sparrow; largely black and white with a *black crown, face, and throat.* The sexes are similar. Young birds may have the black incomplete or confined to a large black splotch across the breast. The black bib suggests no other species except the male House Sparrow, which, of course, could hardly be confused with it.

WHITE-CROWNED SPARROW. *Zonotrichia leucophrys leucophrys.*

Adults: — Breast clear pearly-gray; crown high and puffy, *broadly striped with black and white.* The White-throated Sparrow is striped similarly on the crown, but, in addition, sports a conspicuous white throat. It is, on the whole, a much browner-looking bird.

Immature birds are buffier, with head-stripings of dark red-brown and light buffy-brown instead of black and white, and have pinkish bills. Young White-throats would have the white throat-patch and a touch of yellow before the eye.

GAMBEL'S SPARROW. *Zonotrichia leucophrys gambeli.*

Casual in the East; adult like the White-crown, but the white eye-stripe *starts from the bill,* instead of near the eye. (Do not confuse with White-throat, which also has stripe starting from bill.)

GOLDEN-CROWNED SPARROW. *Zonotrichia coronata.*

Accidental in the East; adult like a White-crowned Sparrow, with *no white line over the eye,* and a *golden-yellow,* instead of white, stripe through the center of the crown. Immature birds look like large female House Sparrows with a yellowish suffusion on the crown.

WHITE-THROATED SPARROW. *Zonotrichia albicollis.*

Clear-breasted with a *white throat-patch* and a *striped black and white crown.* The abrupt white throat, and the *yellow* on the eye-line between bill and eye, distinguish it from the White-crowned Sparrow.

Immature birds, though duller, retain all the essential recognition-marks of the adults.

The Swamp Sparrow has a white throat, too, but a *reddish* crown.

Fox Sparrow. *Passerella iliaca iliaca.*

Large for a Sparrow, larger than a House Sparrow; rich brown, with a *bright rufous-red tail,* conspicuous when the bird flies.

The Hermit Thrush flashes a similar red tail in flight, but is more olive-brown on the back, thin-billed, and *spotted* on the breast, not *streaked.*

Lincoln's Sparrow. *Melospiza lincolni lincolni.*

Like a Song Sparrow, with a shorter tail; streakings on the under parts *much finer* and not aggregated into a large central spot; best identified by a *broad band of pale buff* across the breast.

The buffy band and fine breast streakings separate it from all except the immature Swamp and Song Sparrows. It is grayer-backed than either of those two with a more contrastingly-striped crown. A narrow *eye-ring* is also quite characteristic. The immature Swamp Sparrow during the spring migration is continually misidentified as the Lincoln's Sparrow.

Swamp Sparrow. *Melospiza georgiana.*

A rather stout, dark Sparrow, with a clear-gray breast, a white throat and a *reddish cap*; frequents cat-tail marshes, bushy swamps, etc.

The Chipping Sparrow is clear-breasted with a red cap, but is much less robust and shows a contrasting white stripe over the eye. Field and Tree Sparrows both show prominent wing-bars.

Juvenile Swamp Sparrows are buffy below with fine breast-streakings. They are difficult to distinguish from young Song Sparrows, but are usually darker on the back and redder on the wings. In the hand, a point of absolute certainty (of value to bird-banders) is the color of the inside of the mouth, which in young Swamp Sparrows is largely yellow and in Song Sparrows, pink or gray.

Immature birds in the first winter resemble adults but are not red on the crown.

EASTERN SONG SPARROW. *Melospiza melodia melodia.*
Breast heavily streaked, the streaks confluent into a *large central spot; pumps its tail* as it flies.
The Savannah Sparrow, though streaked similarly below, shows yellow over the eye and has a shorter, *forked* tail. The tail of the Song Sparrow is *rounded.*
Young birds are more finely streaked, without the central spot. (See Lincoln's Sparrow and young Swamp Sparrow.)
ATLANTIC SONG SPARROW. *Melospiza melodia atlantica.*
Paler and grayer; resident of the coastal strips and the edge of the mainland from Long Island to North Carolina.
MISSISSIPPI SONG SPARROW. *Melospiza melodia beata.*
Mississippi Valley.

LAPLAND LONGSPUR. *Calcarius lapponicus lapponicus.*
Longspurs, like Snow Buntings and Horned Larks, are cold-weather birds of the beaches, fields, and barren grounds; like those two they *walk or run*, never hop. The Lapland Longspur is the only common Eastern species.
With Snow Buntings it appears as a smaller, House-Sparrow-like bird, with *dark wings;* when with Horned Larks it can be recognized by the short, Sparrow bill, and the lack of an outlined yellow throat, and on the wing by the *smaller tail* and more undulating flight. Alone, it appears a trifle like a House Sparrow, but *walks or creeps,* does not hop. Two white wing-bars, some narrow black streakings on the sides, and a varying amount of reddish on the nape of the neck are distinctive points. In the spring both sexes acquire a black throat.
The note of a Lapland Longspur amongst a flock of Larks or Buntings is a dry rattling call that can be detected immediately.

SMITH'S LONGSPUR. *Calcarius pictus.*
East in migration to Illinois and southwestern Indiana.
A *buffy* Longspur; a little like the Lapland, but with warm buff on the entire under surface. The male in spring is marked

on the cheek with a white spot strikingly outlined with a triangle of black (in other words, a black auricular patch with a white spot in the center); no other bird is marked similarly.

Chestnut-collared Longspur. *Calcarius ornatus.*

Accidental in the East; the smallest of the Longspurs — considerably smaller than a House Sparrow; known from the other two Longspurs by the large amount of *white* on the sides of the tail. The white in the tail might lead one to confuse it with the Vesper Sparrow or the Pipit. The short thick bill as in the Sparrow, in connection with the *walking* gait of the Pipit, would be conclusive. The tail is considerably shorter than that of either of those two.

The *male* in breeding plumage would be *solid black below* except on the throat.

Snow Bunting. *Plectrophenax nivalis nivalis.*

The great amount of white distinguishes the Snow Bunting. Some individuals look quite brown as they creep or run about, but the moment they spring into the air the extensive white wing-patches flash forth. From below, as they fly overhead, they look almost entirely white; Pipits and Horned Larks are both black-tailed.

HOME–REFERENCE SUGGESTIONS

This handbook is primarily a field guide. *Portraits of New England Birds*, obtainable at the State House in Boston, is recommended as a companion volume for home use. No finer series of bird-portraits exists at the present time. The plates of *The Birds of New York*, distributed by the New York State Museum at Albany, are also very fine. Both are very reasonable and highly useful to bird-students living anywhere in the Northeast.

The volumes from which these plates have been taken are *The Birds of Massachusetts and Other New England States* (3 volumes), by E. H. Forbush, and *The Birds of New York* (2 volumes), by E. H. Eaton. These give, besides the plates, text on life-history, exact status, nesting, etc. For the Mid-West the best existing work is *Birds of Minnesota*, by T. S. Roberts (University of Minnesota Press, Minneapolis); for the South, *Florida Bird Life*, by A. H. Howell (Department of Game and Fresh Water Fish, Tallahassee, Florida). *The Birds of Western Pennsylvania*, by W. E. Clyde Todd (Carnegie Museum, Pittsburgh), is at the present writing in preparation and promises to be very useful to students in the Great Lakes area. For general reference covering the entire East, Chapman's *Handbook of Birds of Eastern North America* (D. Appleton-Century Company) is quite indispensable.

Publications and regional lists of local interest have been published by the following clubs and organizations:

Canadian Geological Survey, Ottawa
Natural History Society of New Brunswick
Nova Scotia Institute of Arts and Sciences
Nuttall Ornithological Club, Cambridge, Massachusetts
Boston Society of Natural History
Vermont State Board of Agriculture
Manchester (New Hampshire) Institute of Arts and Sciences
State Geological Survey, Connecticut
Linnæan Society of New York

Roosevelt Wild-Life Station, University of Syracuse
Cornell University, Department of Ornithology, Ithaca, New York
Buffalo Academy of Sciences
Delaware Valley Ornithological Club, Philadelphia
Reading (Pennsylvania) Public Museum and Art Gallery
Ohio State Division of Conservation
Department of Fish and Game, West Virginia
Department of Fish and Game, Nashville, Tennessee
Charleston (South Carolina) Museum
Indiana Horticultural Society
Illinois Audubon Society, Chicago
Chicago Academy of Sciences
Kansas Academy of Sciences
St. Louis Academy of Sciences
Davenport Academy of Sciences
Wisconsin Society of Natural History

INDEX